DONALD J. SOBOL

Solve the Mystery
and
Improve Your English Skills 3

ミステリーを読んで英語のスキルアップ３

Edited with Notes by

Toshiko Yoshimura
Yukari Tokioka
Susan E. Jones
Mikiko Hirata
Jennifer Teeter
Kayoko Ito

EIHŌSHA

本書籍は、平成 30 年 6 月 25 日に著作権法第 67 条第 1 項の裁定を受け作成したものです。

はしがき

　本テキストは好評の『ミステリーを読んで英語のスキルアップ』シリーズの第3作目です。このシリーズでは Sobol 作のジュニア用短編ミステリーを選択しました。近年、読書離れの傾向もあり、学生たちが文学作品に親しむ機会は少なくなっています。このような潮流のため、大学の英語授業で文学が取り上げられる機会も減っています。しかし、リライトされていないオリジナルの文学作品は、英語学習者にとっての学習素材の宝庫でもあります。学生たちは英語の文学作品に親しみ、生の英語に触れる第一歩として、気軽に楽しく取り組むことができます。これらのミステリーを読みすすめることで、総合的な英語力を高めることができます。

　第1作目はオーセンティックな文学素材を用いて、主にリーディング力を高めることを主眼に、企画・編集されました。第2作目は前テキストに対する現場の先生方からのフィードバックを反映させ、英語の4技能に加えて、学生の苦手意識が強い文法の復習と定着を図ることを目指しました。

　第3作目である本テキストには、前2作での謎解きを英語で書く作業の中で、学習者の発信能力を養成する必要性を痛感したため、アカデミック・ライティング・スキルを学習するセクションを設けました。ライティングの基礎であるレトリックの理解から始め、論理的に説得力のある首尾一貫した英文でエッセイが書けることを目指しています。

　本書は 15 のユニットと、5 ユニットごとに設けた TOEIC 形式のリスニング問題と語彙・文法問題から成る Review Test で構成されています。
　Warm-up は、各ユニットのストーリーに関連する文化事象・言語表現を紹介するとともに、本文のミステリーを解くためのヒントを含む導入部です。
　Pre-reading Section として、本文の理解を助けるため Key Vocabulary と Vocabulary Exercise が用意されています。学習者は Warm-up と併せて、ここで取り上げられた語彙に注意しながら本文を読みすすめることができます。
　Mystery Reading は、学習者の関心、レベルに応じて、柔軟な取り組みが可能です。読み進みやすくなるための注がつけられています。上級レベルでは、Pre-reading Section での語彙のヒントを活かして、速読やスキミングを行ってもよいでしょう。
　Post-reading Section は、まず内容の理解を助けるための T/F (True or False) 問題と Comprehension Questions があります。次に本文のサマリーにもなっている Dictation 問題を設けました。ここでは話の流れを把握するとともに、リ

スニング力の向上を図ることができます。

　次に、Mystery Solving があります。ここでは、それまでの過程を通して理解したミステリーの謎解きを英語で書いてみます。これは文法にあまりこだわらず、伝える内容を重視した実践的な学生の発信能力を高めるためのアクティビティです。また本文の最後のミステリーに関する質問の解答が難しい場合には、本文を精読したり、グループで話し合ったりして、解決の糸口を見つけ出す努力をします。謎解きのプロセスについては、英語で口頭発表をしたり、クラス全員で議論をしたりすることもできます。各自で英語レポートとして要約する方法もあるでしょう。

　最後に「ちょっと一息」からはライティング・スキルを練習するセクションで、2作目の出版以来、現場の先生方からのフィードバックの声を反映させ今回設けました。ライティングの基礎であるパラグラフ・ライティングからエッセイ・ライティングへと段階的に学べるように 15 ユニットで簡潔に提示されています。さまざまなレトリックを認識し、理解するための練習問題、実際にそのレトリックを用いて英文を書く練習からなっています。

　ミステリー作品も日々のコミュニケーションも、同じ言葉によって成り立っています。本テキストの各セクションでの取り組みを通して、学習者が言葉の働きについて考えるきっかけをつかみ、コミュニケーションの基礎となる英語での発信力が高まることを願っています。そして本テキストが、みなさんの英語力の向上に役立ち、さらには文学作品を楽しく読むきっかけとなれば幸いです。

　最後に、本書の刊行にあたり、ライティング部分に関して貴重なご教示をいただいた Thomas Kirchner 氏、的確なご助言と多大なご尽力をいただいた英宝社の佐々木元社長および編集担当の下村幸一氏に、編注者一同、心より感謝致します。

　2018 年秋

編注者一同

CONTENTS

Unit 1 The Case of the Hitchhiker ···················· 1
        Let's Get Started! Understanding Rhetoric

Unit 2 The Case of the Lookout ···················· 5
        Understanding the Paragraph

Unit 3 The Case of the Spilled Brandy ···················· 9
        Writing a Paragraph

Unit 4 The Case of the Locked Wine Cellar ···················· 13
        Expressing Time Order

Unit 5 The Case of the Silk Mantle ···················· 17
        Using Space Order

        Review Test 1 ···················· 21

Unit 6 The Case of the Home Bakery ···················· 23
        Explaining Processes and Giving Directions

Unit 7 The Case of the Cave Paintings ···················· 29
        Giving Examples

Unit 8 The Case of the Lakeside Murder ···················· 33
        Writing Definitions

Unit 9 The Case of the Hero Dog ···················· 37
        Classification

Unit10 The Case of the Million-to-One Shot ···················· 41
        Comparison

        Review Test 2 ···················· 45

Unit11 The Case of the Missing Button ···················· 47
        Contrast

Unit12 The Case of the Gold Brick ···················· 51
        Describing Cause and Effect

Unit13 The Case of the Dying Brazilian ···················· 55
        Developing Paragraphs into Essays

Unit14 The Case of the Stranded Blonde ···················· 61
        Writing an Essay: Using Internet Resources

Unit15 The Case of the Purse Snatcher ···················· 65
        Writing an Argumentative Essay

Review Test 3 69

Appendix 1 Writing Guide: Format, Transitions & Punctuation 71
Appendix 2 How to Organize an Effective Essay Outline 74
Appendix 3 Quotation Usage, Avoiding Plagiarism & Citation Methods 76
Appendix 4 Self-checklists 79

Unit 1
The Case of the Hitchhiker

Warm-up

hitchhiker: ヒッチハイクをする人のことをいいます。hitchhike は hitch（移動する）+ hike（歩いて行く）を合わせた語で、道端に立って通り過ぎる車に乗せてくれるようにお願いすることです。ヒッチハイクを求めるときは手で合図をします。道路に向かって腕を伸ばし、手のひらを閉じて親指を上に突き出したり、ジェスチャーで知らせたりします。看板を掲げる人もいます。見知らぬ人の車に乗せてもらうのですから、気をつけましょう。

Key Vocabulary　語句の意味を下のリストから選びましょう。

1) lift （　） 2) arrest （　） 3) grin （　） 4) relief （　）
5) chase （　） 6) head (*v.*) （　） 7) swing （　） 8) peel （　）
9) shine （　） 10) snap （　）

a) 安堵、安心	b) 進む	c) 光る、輝く	d) 人にきつく言う
e) にこりと笑う、にやりとする	f) 〜の皮をむく	g) 車に乗せること	h) ぐるっと回す
i) 追跡する	j) 逮捕する		

Vocabulary Exercise　Key Vocabulary の中から適当な語句を選びましょう。必要なら形を変えて完成文を訳しましょう。

1) The train was (　　) for Boston.
   _____

2) The police will (　　) the man for two bank robberies.
   _____

3) Could you give me a (　　) to the airport?
   _____

4) He (　　) when he heard the good news.
   _____

5) To my great (　　), he returned home safe.
   _____

Unit 1　　1

Mystery Reading

"Boy, thanks for the lift," exclaimed the young man as he slid off his knapsack and climbed into the front seat of the air-conditioned patrol car beside Sheriff Monahan. "Say, aren't you going to arrest me for bumming a ride?"

"Not today," replied the sheriff. "Too busy."

The young man grinned in relief. He took a chocolate bar from his knapsack, broke off a piece, and offered the rest to the sheriff.

"No, thanks," said the police officer, accelerating the car.

"You chasing someone?" asked the hitchhiker.

"Four men just held up the First National Bank. They escaped in a big black sedan."

"Hey," gasped the hitchhiker. "I saw a black sedan about ten minutes ago. It had four men in it. They nearly ran me off the road. First car I saw in an hour. But they took a left turn. They're headed west, not north."

Sheriff Monahan braked the patrol car and swung it around. The young man began peeling an orange, putting the rinds tidily into a paper bag.

"Look at the heat shining off the road ahead," said the sheriff. "Must be eighty-five in the shade today."

"Must be," agreed the hitchhiker. "Wait—you passed the turnoff—where're you going?"

"To the police station," snapped the sheriff—a decision to which Haledjian heartily agreed upon hearing the hitchhiker's story.

(225 語)

HOW COME?

〈注〉
sheriff: 保安官　　**bum:** ねだる　　**break off:** 折り取る
hold up: ～を襲って強奪する　　**gasp:** あえぎながら言う　　**eighty-five:** 85°F、華氏 85 度（29.4°C）
rind:（果物・野菜などの）皮　　**turnoff:** わき道

True or False

1) The patrol car's air conditioner broke down on the freeway.　　　T/F
2) A young man explained where he wanted to go.　　　T/F
3) Four men robbed the First National Bank.　　　T/F
4) The black sedan ran over the hitchhiker who was rescued by the sheriff.　　　T/F
5) The sheriff arrested the young man for hitchhiking.　　　T/F

Comprehension Questions

1) What did the young man try to give the sheriff?
___

2) How was the weather on the day of the bank robbery?
___

Summary Dictation

Sheriff Monahan ①(　　) up a young hitchhiker. The hitchhiker took a chocolate bar from his knapsack, ②(　　) off a piece and tried to give the ③(　　) to the sheriff. The sheriff told him that four men ④(　　) the First National Bank and went away in a black sedan. Hearing that, the hitchhiker said that he saw a black sedan and there were four men in it. The sheriff said that it was 85 °F in the ⑤(　　) and he headed for the police station.

Mystery Solving

このミステリーの謎解きをしてみましょう。
グループで話し合って謎を解き、英語で書いてみましょう。

<ちょっと一息>

このコーナーでは英文を書くときに必要な英語の *rhetoric* について考えてみましょう。日本人が英語で書いた文章、特に論文やレポートなどは、英語のネイティブ・スピーカーには、その主張や要点がよく理解されないことがあります。Kaplan（1966）は図を用いて、日本語と英語で書かれた文の論理の展開の違いを説明しています。英語では論理が直線的（linear）であるのに対し、東洋系（Oriental）の論理の展開は渦巻きのようになっています。Oriental に含まれる日本語の文章では結論になかなか達せずに論理が婉曲的であることを示しています。
（Kaplan, 1966 より）

English　　　Oriental

 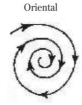

Let's Get Started! Understanding Rhetoric

Exercise 1

自由に英語を書いてみましょう。10分間で一語でも多く英語を書いてください。テーマは"My Hometown"です。書き終えたら総単語数を数えましょう。

Exercise 2

次の日本語の意味に合う単語を選びましょう。

1) 学部 　　　　　　　　　　　　　a) easygoing
2) 専攻（する）　　　　　　　　　b) graduate
3) 将来の目標　　　　　　　　　　c) part-time job
4) 大学2年生　　　　　　　　　　d) outgoing
5) 卒業する　　　　　　　　　　　e) future goal
6) 好きな活動　　　　　　　　　　f) college sophomore
7) 社交的な　　　　　　　　　　　g) faculty
8) アルバイト　　　　　　　　　　h) favorite activity
9) のんきな　　　　　　　　　　　i) countryside
10) 田舎　　　　　　　　　　　　　j) major（in）

Exercise 3

次の英文に続けて自己紹介文を50語程度で書きましょう。

　　Let me introduce myself. My name is _____. Please call me

_____. _____

_____

_____

_____

_____

_____

Unit 2
The Case of the Lookout

Warm-up

nun: 修道女、尼僧のことです。キリスト教では修道女は"sister"とも呼ばれ、清貧、貞潔、服従の三つの修道請願を立て、修道院で黙想、祈りの共同生活を送ります。世俗の職業を持つことは基本的になく、俗世間とは離れた生活を送ります。また仏教の尼僧は出家して仏門に入った女性です。

Key Vocabulary 語句の意味を下のリストから選びましょう。

1) chauffeur (　)　　2) sip (*n.*) (　)　　3) upset (　)　　4) bullet (　)
5) dash (　)　　6) barely (　)　　7) customer (　)　　8) refuge (　)
9) remove (　)　　10) depart (　)

a) ひとすすり、ひと口	b) 逃げ場	c) 動揺した、狼狽した	d) わずかに、かろうじて
e) 銃弾	f) 顧客	g) 突進する	h) 取り去る、持ち去る
i) お抱え運転手	j) 出発する		

Vocabulary Exercise
Key Vocabulary の中から適当な語句を選びましょう。必要なら形を変えて完成文を訳しましょう。

1) A (　　　) is a person who buys goods or services from a shop.
   _____

2) Don't (　　　) the magazine from the desk.
   _____

3) He was terribly (　　　) to read the letter.
   _____

4) He suddenly (　　　) for England yesterday.
   _____

5) She took another (　　　) of wine before going to bed.
   _____

Mystery Reading

Dr. Haledjian was the only customer in the little drugstore when the shooting started.

He had just taken his first sip of black coffee when three men dashed from the bank across the street, guns blazing.

As the holdup men jumped into a waiting car, a nun and a chauffeur sought refuge in the drugstore.

"You're both upset," said Haledjian. "Let me buy you a cup of coffee."

They thanked him. The nun ordered black coffee, the chauffeur a glass of root beer.

The three fell to talking about the flying bullets and had barely touched their drinks when sirens sounded.

The robbers had been captured and were being returned to the bank for identification.

Haledjian moved to a front window to watch. As he returned to the counter, the nun and chauffeur thanked him again and departed.

The counterman had cleared the glass and cups. "Sorry, mister," he said to Haledjian. "I didn't know you weren't done."

The counterman looked at the two coffee cups he had just removed from the counter, and passing Haledjian the one without lipstick, said, "What do you think a chauffeur was doing around here? There isn't a limousine on the street."

Haledjian thought a moment. "Good grief!" he cried. "We had the gang's lookout right here!"

And he dashed out to make the capture.

(225 語)

WHAT AROUSED HALEDJIAN'S SUSPICION?

〈注〉
blaze: 銃が乱射される   **holdup:** 強盗
root beer: ルートビア（ササフラスの木の根や皮などに香をつけた、コーラに似た甘い炭酸飲料。見かけはビールに似ているがノンアルコール飲料）
good grief: 非常に残念なこと   **lookout:** 見張り

6   The Case of the Lookout

True or False

1) A nun came in the drugstore to buy a cup of coffee. T/F
2) Dr. Haledjian had not finished his coffee when the nun and the chauffeur left the drugstore. T/F
3) The nun and the chauffeur were arrested in the drugstore. T/F
4) At first, Dr. Haledjian was not suspicious of the nun and the chauffeur. T/F
5) The bank robbers tried to get onto the train. T/F

Comprehension Questions

1) What did Dr. Haledjian offer the nun and chauffeur?

2) How many customers were there in the drugstore before the shooting?

Summary Dictation

Dr. Haledjian was drinking coffee in the drugstore at the time of the ①(　　　). A nun and a chauffeur came in the drugstore seeking ②(　　　). Dr. Haledjian tried to buy the two people a cup of coffee. The nun ordered black coffee and the ③(　　　) a glass of root beer. The ④(　　　) were caught and the two left the drugstore. The counterman ⑤(　　　) Dr. Haledjian the coffee cup without lipstick. Dr. Haledjian found out that he and the counterman had met the gang's lookout.

Mystery Solving

このミステリーの謎解きをしてみましょう。
グループで話し合って謎を解き、英語で書いてみましょう。

＜ちょっと一息＞

英文の paragraph（パラグラフ）について考えてみましょう。パラグラフは、通常、1つのトピックやアイデアについて複数の文から構成される基本的な単位です。Topic sentence（トピック・センテンス）で始まることが多く、その後に supporting sentences（サポーティング・センテンス）が続き、最後に concluding sentence（コンクルーディング・センテンス）がきます。

Unit 2　7

Understanding the Paragraph

Exercise 1

パラグラフの形を学びましょう。パラグラフの最初はインデントをし、3〜5文字分をあけて書き出します。

3〜5文字分インデントする

トピック・センテンス	メイン・アイディア（主語）
サポーティング・センテンス	メイン・アイディアを支持する文
コンクルーディング・センテンス	トピック・センテンスと同じ内容を、少し言葉を変えて述べる結論文

Exercise 2

次の英文を読んで下の問いに答えましょう。

Differences in British and American Spelling

(1) British and American English have some minor differences in spelling. (2) Where British English uses "-our," as in the words "colour" or "neighbour," American spelling usually leaves out the "u" (color, neighbor). (3) Some words that end in "-er" in American usage, such as center and meter, have the final two letters reversed in British English (centre, metre). (4) Finally, Americans often use "-se" where Britons use "-ce"; "defense" (American) versus "defence" (British) is a characteristic example. (5) Although these differences are small, they are important to remember.

1) トピック・センテンスを選びましょう。（　　）

2) サポーティング・センテンスを選びましょう。（　　）（　　）（　　）

3) コンクルーディング・センテンスを選びましょう。（　　）

Exercise 3

次のトピックに関して、例を参考にしてコメントを補いトピック・センテンスを書いてみましょう。

（例）My favorite drink <u>is orange juice.</u>

1. Part-time jobs _____

2. My university _____

3. Smartphones _____

4. An unforgettable memory _____

Unit 3
The Case of the Spilled Brandy

Warm-up

farmhouse: 田園地帯、農村地帯にある農場、農家の母屋のことです。アメリカのfarmhouse は、すっきりした構造で農場の真ん中に建てられます。床の形状はシンプルな長方形です。

upstate: 州北部のことを言いますが、特にNew York 州の北部の都会から離れた田舎を指します。ワシントン・アービング作の物語 *Rip Van Winkle* はこの辺りの The Catskill Mountains が舞台になっています。

Key Vocabulary　語句の意味を下のリストから選びましょう。

1) spill　　　(　)　2) apologize　(　)　3) stuff　　(　)　4) recall　(　)
5) burst out　(　)　6) awfully　　(　)　7) disappear (　)　8) steady　(　)
9) emphatic　(　)　10) unexpectedly (　)

a) 謝る	b) 急に飛び出す	c) もの、飲み物	d) 姿を消す
e) 落ち着かせる	f) 思いがけなく	g) 語気の強い	h) こぼす
i) 非常に	j) 思い出す		

Vocabulary Exercise　Key Vocabulary の中から適当な語句を選びましょう。必要なら形を変えて完成文を訳しましょう。

1) This new invention was not entirely (　　　).

2) He (　　　) for his bad behavior yesterday.

3) "At that time, we were going to take the train," John (　　　).

4) He (　　　) behind the garden gate on that day.

5) He was (　　　) about the important point.

Mystery Reading

In pouring Dr. Haledjian's 20-year-old brandy, Inspector Winters inadvertently spilled a liberal quantity on the carpet. He apologized and chuckled reminiscently. "Last year I arrested a man after he'd spilled some brandy—and not nearly such good stuff as this, either."

"So?" said Haledjian inquiringly.

"I was driving upstate for the weekend," recalled the inspector. "Somehow, I took a wrong turn. I pulled up to a big farmhouse to ask directions.

"As I stopped my car behind a black convertible in the driveway, a young man burst out of the house.

"'Do you live here?' he shouted excitedly.

"I told him I didn't. Nonetheless he seemed awfully glad to have somebody else around. He said he was a stranger who'd stopped to ask directions a minute before I arrived.

"'The house is empty—except for a woman lying on the sofa. I th-think she's dead!' he exclaimed.

"The woman wasn't dead, but she wasn't very alive. Not with her head bloody and bruises on her throat. I told the excited young man to find some brandy, and he disappeared into the kitchen while I telephoned the police.

"When the young man came back, I tried to tell him the brandy was to steady his nerves. But he acted too swiftly. He put the bottle to the unconscious woman's lips. He'd spilled most of it over her chin and throat before I yanked the bottle away.

"'Leave her alone!' I ordered. And just to make it emphatic, I held my gun on him till the local police could place him under arrest. Luckily, the girl survived. But if I hadn't driven up unexpectedly, he'd have finished choking her to death."

(286 語)

HOW DID THE INSPECTOR KNOW?

〈注〉
inadvertently: うっかり
reminiscently: 昔をなつかしんで
except for: 〜は別として、除いて
yank: グイッと引っ張る
liberal: たくさんの
inquiringly: 聞きたそうに
exclaim: 叫ぶ
choke: 窒息死させる
chuckle: くすくす笑う
convertible: オープンカー
bruise: 挫傷、打撲傷

True or False

1) When Winters spilled Dr. Haledjian's brandy, he recalled the case.   T/F
2) While Winters was driving, he wanted to find a way to the beach.   T/F
3) Winters was not very familiar with the upstate area.   T/F
4) A young man saw a beautiful apartment, and he wished he could live there.   T/F
5) Unfortunately, a woman was found dead near the farm gate.   T/F

Comprehension Questions

1) Why did Winters stop at a big farmhouse?

2) Where was the woman lying?

Summary Dictation

When Winters stopped at a farmhouse to ask the way, he saw a young man ①(   ) out of the house. He said a woman was ②(   ). Winters and the man came into the house and found the woman, who was barely ③(   ). The man said that he had never visited the house. Winters asked the man to ④(   ) some brandy. He came back from the kitchen with the brandy. Winters realized that the man should be under ⑤(   ).

Mystery Solving

このミステリーの謎解きをしてみましょう。
グループで話し合って謎を解き、英語で書いてみましょう。

＜ちょっと一息＞

ここではパラグラフを書いてみましょう。英語では、パラグラフがひとつのまとまりのある考えを表す最小単位です。普通は、最初の行を3〜5文字下げて書き始めます。その中には必ず、topic sentence（トピック・センテンス）と、主題をサポートする supporting sentences（サポーティング・センテンス）が含まれています。最後に concluding sentence（コンクルーディング・センテンス）を書き、パラグラフを締めくくります。

Unit 3   11

Writing a Paragraph

Exercise 1

Appendix 1 を見てパラグラフの型を学習しましょう。

Exercise 2

"The Charm of Tokyo"（東京の魅力）について、旅行者の立場から (2), (3), (4) に英文を入れ書いてみましょう。

The Charm of Tokyo

3〜5文字分インデントする
↓

トピック・センテンス	1) Tokyo has many things for travelers to do.
サポーティング・センテンス	2)
サポーティング・センテンス	3)
サポーティング・センテンス	4)
コンクルーディング・センテンス	5) No matter what the travelers' taste, Tokyo has something to offer.

Exercise 3

"Places I Want to Visit"（行ってみたい場所）について、one paragraph で書いてみましょう。
（50 語以上）

Places I Want to Visit

_____

_____

_____

_____

_____

_____

Unit 4
The Case of the Locked Wine Cellar

Warm-up

wine cellar: ワイン貯蔵室のことです。この部屋では温度や湿度が制御され、ワインにとって最適な状態が保たれます。最適な温度は約13度ぐらいです。湿度が低すぎるとコルクが乾燥してボトルとの間に隙間が出来て、ボトルの中に空気が入りワインを劣化させます。50%～70%程度の湿度が適しています。また太陽光線はワインの品質を劣化させます。そのためにワインは色ガラスのボトルに入れられています。

Key Vocabulary　語句の意味を下のリストから選びましょう。

1) inquire　（　）　　2) dim　（　）　　3) theft　（　）　　4) slip　（　）
5) invariably　（　）　6) safe　（　）　7) adequate　（　）　8) cast　（　）
9) inspect　（　）　10) basement　（　）

a) 尋ねる	b) 調べる	c) ほの暗い	d) しくじり、あやまち
e) 適切な、妥当な	f) 地下室	g) 常に、必ず	h) 金庫
i) 盗み、窃盗	j)（光などを）放つ、投げかける		

Vocabulary Exercise　Key Vocabulary の中から適当な語句を選びましょう。必要なら形を変えて完成文を訳しましょう。

1) When the burglar broke in, he hid in the (　　　).

2) The (　　　) street lights were on, but it was a dark evening.

3) She keeps her jewelry in a (　　　) in the bedroom.

4) All cars were stopped and carefully (　　　) by the police.

5) The moonlight (　　　) a bright glow on the street that night.

Unit 4　　13

Mystery Reading

Because Wentworth Boyd invariably caught the 9:53 express Friday morning and arrived at his country home exactly two hours later, Dr. Haledjian was able to solve the theft of $50,000 from Boyd's wall safe.

One Friday, Boyd broke his habit without advising anyone. On this day he arrived home shortly before midnight and found his front door ajar. Down in the basement, locked in the wine cellar, he heard his secretary, Nigel Arbuter, shouting for help.

"Coming!" cried Boyd.

"Mr. Boyd!" called Arbuter. "Robbers. I heard them say they'd catch the midnight train back to New York City!"

Boyd freed Arbuter, telephoned the police, and drove to the station. Too late. The train had already pulled out, foiling the police as well.

Dr. Haledjian, at Boyd's request, made his investigation the next day.

"You say two masked robbers forced you at gunpoint to unlock the safe?" he inquired.

"That's right," said Arbuter. "Then they forced a pill—some sort of sleeping potion— down my throat. I awoke in the wine cellar just before Mr. Boyd came downstairs."

Haledjian inspected the wine cellar, a windowless room 13 feet by 9 feet. The door locked from the outside. A single 40-watt bulb cast dim but adequate illumination.

Haledjian looked down at Arbuter's wristwatch. "Were you wearing it at the time of the robbery?"

"Why, y-yes," replied the secretary.

"Then kindly tell us where you hid the money you helped steal!" Haledjian ordered.

(246 語)

WHAT WAS ARBUTER'S SLIP?

〈注〉
ajar: 少し開いて **pull out**: (列車などが) 出ていく **foil**: くじく、挫折させる
at gunpoint: 銃をつきつけられて **illumination**: 照明

The Case of the Locked Wine Cellar

True or False

1) When Boyd came home, the front door was open.　　　　　　　　T/F
2) Dr. Haledjian helped Boyd rescue Arbuter from the wine cellar.　　T/F
3) Arbuter insisted that he was forced to open the safe.　　　　　　T/F
4) The wine cellar had a very small window.　　　　　　　　　　　T/F
5) Dr. Haledjian was Boyd's close friend.　　　　　　　　　　　　T/F

Comprehension Questions

1) What was the train that Boyd always caught?
_____

2) What was taken from the safe?
_____

Summary Dictation

Boyd always ①(　　　) the same train in the morning and arrived at his country home around noon. However, on that day, Boyd broke his ②(　　　) and came home shortly before midnight. He found that Arbuter was ③(　　　) in the wine cellar. Arbuter ④(　　　) that two masked robbers stole money out of the safe and they forced him to take a sleeping pill. He woke in the wine cellar just before Boyd came ⑤(　　　). Haledjian found that Arbuter was wearing a wristwatch and told him to confess where he hid the money.

Mystery Solving

このミステリーの謎解きをしてみましょう。
グループで話し合って謎を解き、英語で書いてみましょう。

＜ちょっと一息＞

Time order の *rhetoric*（時間の順序）について練習してみましょう。Time order は chronological order とも呼ばれ、出来事の起こった順、あるいは、これから起こるだろうと想定する順、時間の経過にそって書き進めるものです。出来事や、物語、経験、手順、過程などの描写があります。

Unit 4　　15

Expressing Time Order

Exercise 1

下の単語の意味を右の語群から選びましょう。

1) First,　　　　　(　　　)　　　a. 結局
2) Next,　　　　　(　　　)　　　b. 次の、翌
3) Then 〜　　　　(　　　)　　　c. 〜の時
4) When 〜　　　　(　　　)　　　d. 最後に
5) After 〜　　　　(　　　)　　　e. 〜の後に、
6) Finally,　　　　(　　　)　　　f. そして
7) In the end,　　 (　　　)　　　g. 最初は、はじめに

Exercise 2

下の英文を読んで次の問いに答えましょう。

1. 主題文に下線を引きましょう。
2. (　　　) にタイム・オーダーを示す語句を Exercise 1 から選び、記号で入れましょう。

　　Monday morning was a disaster. It was the day of an important meeting with my boss.
①(　　　) I woke up at 9:00, but I needed to take the 9:30 train. I got dressed quickly.
②(　　　) I rushed to the kitchen to make coffee. ③(　　　) I drank it, I spilled some on my
shirt. ④(　　　) I changed my shirt, I realized I had to leave right away. ⑤(　　　) I grabbed
my bag. ⑥(　　　) I reached my train just in time.

Exercise 3

次の文の（1),（2),（3）から一つ単語を選び、"Yesterday" について英文の続きを書いて、one
paragraphで完成させましょう。

○○○○○ Yesterday was [1) a happy, 2) an unlucky, 3) a sad] day. _____

_____

_____

_____

_____

_____

_____

Unit 5
The Case of the Silk Mantle

Warm-up

fireplace: レンガや石で作られた暖炉のことです。暖炉の上には炉棚、mantel（= mantelshelf）が設けられます。そこには写真や飾り物が置かれ、絵画が飾られることもあります。

homonym: 同音異義語。pail（桶）と pale（青白い）、sea（海）と see（見る）のように発音が同じで意味が異なる語があります。日本語にも「雨（あめ）」と「飴（あめ）」、「花（はな）」と「鼻（はな）」のような例がたくさんあります。文脈をよく考えないとうっかり意味を取り間違えてしまいます。

Key Vocabulary　語句の意味を下のリストから選びましょう。

1) attempt （　）　2) flee （　）　3) notify （　）　4) suspicion （　）
5) false （　）　6) garment （　）　7) chilly （　）　8) ascertain （　）
9) shift （　）　10) urge （　）

a) 疑い、容疑	b) 衣服	c) 試みる	d) 確かめる
e) 偽の	f) 移動させる	g) 通報する、通知する	h) 逃げる
i) 駆り立てる、急きたてる	j) 冷たい、うすら寒い		

Vocabulary Exercise　Key Vocabulary の中から適当な語句を選びましょう。必要なら形を変えて完成文を訳しましょう。

1) The police were (　　) of her motives.

2) They were (　　) to join the marathon.

3) He (　　) his weight from one foot to the other.

4) She was (　　) that her child was missing.

5) When the police arrived at the house, they (　　) to open the door.

Mystery Reading

Police established the following facts:

1. On a beastly hot day, a masked man had entered the Cartonses' apartment. In attempting to beat from Mrs. Carton the hiding place of her diamond necklace, he had accidentally killed her. He had ransacked the apartment and fled empty-handed.

2. Mr. Carton, an invalid who had been under sedation during the crime, discovered the body and notified police.

3. Suspicion fell upon Bill, the doorman and an ex-con, who had not reported to work since the slaying.

4. The necklace was safely hidden in the false bottom of a jewelry box in the guest closet near the fireplace. The box rested on the closet shelf above the spot where Mrs. Carton habitually hung her gold silk mantle. She wore this garment in the apartment on chilly days, but never outside the apartment.

Upon ascertaining these facts, Dr. Haledjian asked to be left alone in the apartment with the doorman.

After hearing Bill insist he had never set foot in the apartment, Haledjian shifted a cigarette container and two statuettes on the shelf above the fireplace and rested his elbow there.

"The necklace was right here in the false bottom of a box above the mantle. See for yourself," urged the sleuth. "Come on!"

In a moment, Bill had found the jade box above Mrs. Carton's silk mantle.

After he was clapped under arrest, Haledjian told Inspector Winters, "A criminal should never return to the scene of his crime."

(249 語)

WHAT WAS BILL'S MISTAKE?

〈注〉
ransack: くまなく探す　　**invalid:** 病人　　**be under sedation:** 鎮静剤を与えられている
ex-con: 前科者　　**slaying:** 殺人　　**statuette:** 小像
elbow: ひじ　　**sleuth:** 探偵　　**arrest:** 逮捕する

18　　The Case of the Silk Mantle

True or False

1) Mrs. Carton was lucky enough to survive the attack.　　　　　T/F
2) Mr. Carton was not a healthy and active man.　　　　　　　　T/F
3) A masked man found the necklace and took it.　　　　　　　　T/F
4) Bill insisted that he had never been to the apartment.　　　　T/F
5) Mrs. Carton sometimes walked outdoors wearing the silk mantle.　T/F

Comprehension Questions

1) What kind of day was it when the crime took place?
_____

2) Who was suspected of murder at first?
_____

Summary Dictation

A masked man tried to ①(　　　) the diamond necklace. However, he killed Mrs. Carton and ran away ②(　　　)-handed. The necklace was in a jewelry box which was on the closet shelf above Mrs. Carton's silk mantle. Though Bill was a prime ③(　　　) in the case, he insisted that he had never visited the apartment. Haledjian told Bill to check the jewelry box above the mantle. Then Bill took the ④(　　　) box above Mrs. Carton's silk mantle. That ⑤(　　　) to his arrest.

Mystery Solving

このミステリーの謎解きをしてみましょう。
グループで話し合って謎を解き、英語で書いてみましょう。

＜ちょっと一息＞

Space order の *rhetoric*（空間の配列）について練習してみましょう。風景などの自然描写や部屋の間取り、室内の様子など様々なケースがありますが、読者がその場所に行ったことがなくても、読んでいてよくわかるように書く必要があります。大切なことは、ある視点を定めて「近くから遠くへ」または、「遠くから近くへ」と遠近法で説明したり、時計回り（または逆時計回り）に記述することです。

Using Space Order

Exercise 1
Mystery Reading の本文の中から space order を示す語句を見つけて、書き出しましょう。

1)   2)   3)   4)   5)   6)

Exercise 2
次の絵を見て、下の語句から適語を選び（　　）に入れましょう。文頭にくる語も小文字にしてあります。2 回以上使う語があります。

on, center, clockwise, near, in front of

　　　This is a picture of my living room from the entrance. I will describe it going ①(　　　) around the room. On the left, there is a fireplace with two bottles ②(　　　) top. ③(　　　) the picture, there is a large window with curtains. ④(　　　) the window, there is a desk with a lamp. Also, there is a flower vase ⑤(　　　) the floor beside the desk. Finally, there is a round rug in the ⑥(　　　) of the room. It is a perfect living room for a holiday home.

Exercise 3
① **"My Favorite Place on Campus"** について one paragraph で書きましょう。
②あなたの大学のキャンパスで、お気に入りの場所を写真に撮り説明してください。

My Favorite Place on Campus

3〜5文字分インデントする

トピック・センテンス	1)
サポーティング・センテンス	2)
サポーティング・センテンス	3)
サポーティング・センテンス	4)
コンクルーディング・センテンス	5)

Review Test 1: Unit 1〜Unit 5

▶ I Photographs

1.
2.

(A)   (B)   (C)   (D)   (A)   (B)   (C)   (D)

3.
4.

(A)   (B)   (C)   (D)   (A)   (B)   (C)   (D)

▶ II Question-Response

1) Mark your answer on your answer sheet.   (A)   (B)   (C)
2) Mark your answer on your answer sheet.   (A)   (B)   (C)
3) Mark your answer on your answer sheet.   (A)   (B)   (C)
4) Mark your answer on your answer sheet.   (A)   (B)   (C)
5) Mark your answer on your answer sheet.   (A)   (B)   (C)

▶ III 文法・語彙

1. The city library (　　　) near the city hall.
   a) locate
   b) is locate
   c) is located
   d) be locate

2. I heard her (　　　) on the phone in the living room last night.
   a) to talk
   b) talking
   c) have talked
   d) have talking

3. I visited many places (　　　) my stay in Tokyo.
   a) when
   b) during
   c) as
   d) to

4. We were looking for the house (　　　) my friend lived.
   a) what
   b) which
   c) where
   d) as

5. If the weather (　　　), the flight would not have been canceled.
   a) had been fine
   b) be fine
   c) have been fine
   d) had fine

6. The doctor told him to give up (　　　).
   a) smoke
   b) to smoke
   c) have smoked
   d) smoking

7. She took a picture of her baby (　　　) on the bed.
   a) sleeping
   b) sleep
   c) to sleep
   d) have slept

8. He went down the stairs (　　　) led to the wine cellar.
   a) what
   b) which
   c) to which
   d) where

9. They were badly (　　　) in a traffic accident.
   a) injure
   b) injuring
   c) injured
   d) to injure

10. (　　　) along a beach, I saw a surfer standing on a surfboad.
    a) To walk
    b) Had walked
    c) Walked
    d) Walking

Unit 6
The Case of the Home Bakery

Warm-up

bakery: パン屋、製パン所のことです。パンやケーキなど、オーブンで焼いた小麦粉などをベースにした食物を調理し販売するお店です。飲み物、スープやサンドイッチなどの軽食を販売したり、店内で食事できるカフェを兼ねたところもあります。

Ma: お母ちゃんの意味です。主にアメリカで呼びかけに使われる幼児語で、現在ではPa同様古風になってきています。年配の女性にも使われていました。「大草原の小さな家」に出てくる子供達は両親を"Ma","Pa"と呼んでいます。

Key Vocabulary　語句の意味を下のリストから選びましょう。

1) obediently ( )　2) criminologist ( )　3) dwell ( )　4) bustle ( )
5) brew ( )　6) premises ( )　7) bicarbonate ( )　8) motherly ( )
9) indigestion ( )　10) apologetically ( )

a) 消化不良	b) すまなそうに	c) 重炭酸塩、重曹	d) 母親のような
e) 調合する、いれる	f) 家屋、建物	g) 従順に、素直に	h) 忙しそうに動く
i) 住む	j) 犯罪学者		

Vocabulary Exercise　Key Vocabularyの中から適当な語句を選びましょう。必要なら形を変えて完成文を訳しましょう。

1) My cousin Betty is ( ) to her parents.

_____

2) Would you like to take some medicine for ( )?

_____

3) He ( ) some fresh coffee for the guests.

_____

4) New York City is ( ) with life.

_____

5) Her mother has ( ) in Portland since she was born.

_____

Mystery Reading

"I was driving by when I got the darndest attack of indigestion," said Sheriff Monahan apologetically. "Do you have some bicarbonate of soda?"

Mrs. Duffy, a motherly woman of sixty, smiled cheerfully. "You just sit right down in the kitchen, Sheriff," she said. "I don't keep bicarbonate of soda on hand, but I'll brew you a nice cup of tea. It'll work wonders, I promise."

Sheriff Monahan seated himself obediently while Mrs. Duffy bustled about her neat little kitchen. He had always admired the kindly woman who dwelt alone and made her own living.

After the sheriff had finished his tea, he rose to leave. "I feel better already. Many thanks."

Outside, he saw Mrs. Duffy's panel truck. It was parked by the south wing of the house which, he had always assumed, was her bakery, in which she made the bread, cakes, and pies she sold to inns along the highway.

He studied the pink lettering on the truck: "Ma Duffy's Homemade Pies, Cakes, and Bread." He stared thoughtfully at the house.

Back in town he telephoned Dr. Haledjian. The famed criminologist heartily advised him to get a search warrant, and within the hour the sheriff had returned to Mrs. Duffy's.

A search of the premises disclosed that Ma Duffy's pies, cakes, and bread were commercial products with wrappers removed. But the bottles of whiskey illegally secreted within each Pullman loaf were strictly home brewed.

(236 語)

WHAT MADE THE SHERIFF SUSPICIOUS?

〈注〉
darndest: damnedest（ひどく変わっている；とても驚くべき）の別表記
on hand: 手元に
panel truck: パネルトラック、小型のバン
Pullman loaf: 角型食パン（現在では使われていない表現）
work wonders: 驚くほどよく効く
search warrant: 捜査令状

True or False

1) Dr. Haledjian was driving when he had an attack of indigestion.　T/F
2) Mrs. Duffy served Monahan a special cup of tea.　T/F
3) Dr. Haledjian had always admired Mrs. Duffy who lived alone and made her own living.　T/F
4) Sheriff Monahan advised Dr. Haledjian to get a search warrant.　T/F
5) Mrs. Duffy's house was cleaned by Dr. Haledjian and the police.　T/F

Comprehension Questions

1) How old was Mrs. Duffy at that time?

2) What did they find in each Pullman loaf?

Summary Dictation

Sheriff Monahan had a sudden attack of ①(　　). Instead of going to a ②(　　), he stopped by Mrs. Duffy's bakery to ask for some ③(　　) of soda. Instead, Mrs. Duffy made him a cup of tea and he felt much better. Mrs. Duffy made her own living operating a home bakery. But something made Monahan feel suspicious about it. Haledjian told him to investigate, and his feeling was ④(　　) correct. The Pullman loaves ⑤(　　) more than met the eye!

Mystery Solving

このミステリーの謎解きをしてみましょう。
グループで話し合って謎を解き、英語で書いてみましょう。

＜ちょっと一息＞

ここでは、process and direction の *rhetoric*（物事の過程、手順や道程などを示す文章の展開）を練習してみましょう。どんな場合があるでしょうか。料理などの調理法や取り扱い説明書、道案内などです。物事を正しい順序に並べて、明確な指示文にすることが大切です。

Explaining Processes and Giving Directions

Exercise 1

（　　）に下の選択肢から適語を入れましょう。

a) after   b) final   c) first   d) following   e) next   f) second   g) then   h) third   i) finally

Planning a Vacation

Plan a vacation in five easy steps. The ①(　　) thing you must do is to choose where you want to visit. ②(　　) that, decide when you will go and how you will get there. The ③(　　) step is searching for interesting spots to see. ④(　　), pack your bags and go! The ⑤(　　) step is to enjoy your vacation

Exercise 2

Beef Bowl（牛丼）の作り方を知っていますか。筋が通るように Exercise 1 の（a）～（i）から適語を選び（　　）に入れ、作り方の正しい順に並べ替えましょう。

1. (　　), pour the beef mixture over rice.
2. (　　), add the cut beef to the pot and stir, simmering about 5 minutes.
3. (　　), slice the onions thinly and cut the beef into small pieces.
4. (　　), add soy sauce, sugar, sake and mirin, and cook another 3-4 minutes.
5. (　　), boil dashi in a pot and add the sliced onion.

Exercise 3

友達が駅から電話をしてきました。次頁の地図を見て、あなたの家までの道順を教えましょう。

My apartment is a ten-minute walk from the station. It is on the 5th floor of the Park Tower Building north of the station. _____

_____

_____

_____

_____

_____

_____

【ヒント】（すべて使うとは限りません）

turn right/left   go straight   on the right/left   take the elevator/stairs to
pass the _____   next to   behind   cross _____ street

26   The Case of the Home Bakery

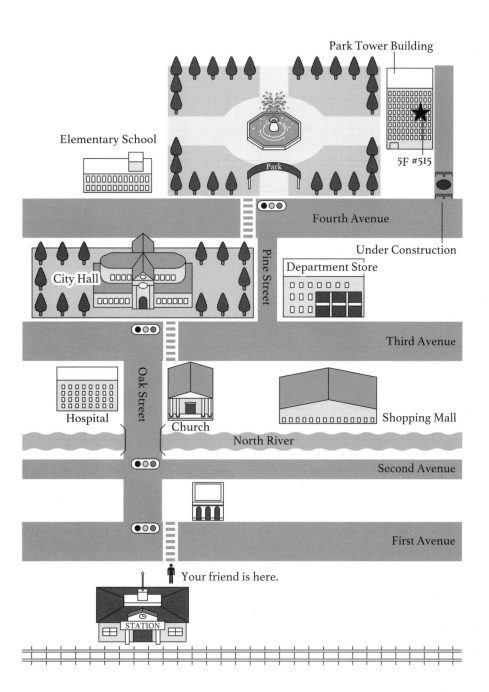

[MEMO]

Unit 7
The Case of the Cave Paintings

Warm-up

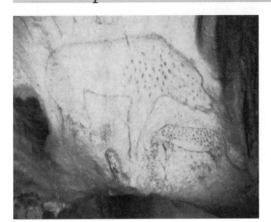

by Carla Hufstedler

cave painting: 洞窟壁画のことで、通例では有史以前の、洞窟や岩壁の壁面や天井部に描かれた絵の総称です。写真は約3万2000年前のショーヴェ洞窟のハイエナの壁画で、現存する人類最古の絵画の一つです。これはネアンデルタール人が作成したもので、oral spray painting（吹き墨）の技法で描かれています。現在は壁画の保護のため、非公開になっています。

Key Vocabulary　語句の意味を下のリストから選びましょう。

1) divulge　　( )　2) subterranean ( )　3) associate　( )　4) behold　　( )
5) prehistoric ( )　6) charge　　( )　7) rhinoceros ( )　8) unemployed ( )
9) caveman　( )　10) woolly　　( )

a) サイ	b) 毛の多い	c) 突進する	d)（石器時代の）穴居人
e) 仲間、友人	f) 先史時代の	g) 秘密を漏らす	h) 地下の
i) 眺める、見る	j) 仕事のない		

Vocabulary Exercise　Key Vocabulary の中から適当な語句を選びましょう。必要なら形を変えて完成文を訳しましょう。

1) Mary has been (　　) for six years due to the big earthquake.

___

2) The big dog suddenly (　　) at me.

___

3) He (　　) the secret of his success.

___

4) We (　　) a bright star shining in the sky.

___

5) Betty has a beautiful (　　) coat.

___

Mystery Reading

"By Jove! This time I'm going to make us both rich!" exclaimed Bertie Tilford, the unemployed Englishman with more get-rich-quick schemes than tail feathers on a turkey farm.

He paused dramatically, eyeing Dr. Haledjian. "You've heard of the cavemen paintings in the Cave of Font de Gaume, France?" he resumed. "Well, my associate, Sebastian Delsolo, has found the greatest ever example of prehistoric art in a cave on a farm in Spain.

"Of course," went on Bertie, "I can't divulge the exact location yet. But we can buy the farm with the cave for a mite, dear boy. The farmer suspects nothing. Think of the fortune from tourists!"

Bertie passed three photos to Haledjian. "Behold! Sebastian pushed past subterranean water channels as far down as four thousand feet to photograph those drawings!"

The first photo was of a drawing of a woolly rhinoceros, the second of hunters attacking a dinosaur, the third of a charging mammoth.

"The cave artist worked by light from a stone lamp filled with fat and fitted with a wick of moss," explained Bertie. "He used pieces of red and yellow ochre for drawing and ground them and mixed them with animal fat for painting."

"How much to buy the farm?" asked Haledjian darkly.

"In American—fifty thousand dollars," said Bertie. "But you can have a third share of everything for a mere ten thousand."

"A third of nothing, you mean," corrected Haledjian. "I won't give you a nickel!"

(244 語)

WHY NOT?

〈注〉
for a mite = for just a little bit (of money), at a low price
fit with: 取り付ける
red ochre: 紅殻(べんがら)
wick of moss: コケをロウソクの芯にした
yellow ochre: 黄土、イエローオーカー

True or False

1) Bertie Tilford was a rich Englishman working in America.   T/F
2) Bertie liked to get feathers on a turkey farm.   T/F
3) Sebastian Delsolo was a friend of Bertie.   T/F
4) Sebastian took pictures as far down as five thousand feet.   T/F
5) The cave artist used red, yellow, and ochre colors for the painting.   T/F

Comprehension Questions

1) What did Sebastian find in Spain?

2) How much did Bertie say it would cost to buy the farm?

Summary Dictation

The ①(   ) Bertie Tilford always has get-rich-quick ideas. This time, he tells Haledjian about some ②(   ) art in a cave in Spain. The cave is on a farm, and the farmer is ③(   ) to sell the land because he doesn't know about the ④(   ) site. Tilford describes the art to Haledjian and offers to let him in on the land ⑤(   ), but Haledjian is suspicious of the story, and doesn't accept the offer. Tilford must keep looking for another path to riches!

Mystery Solving

このミステリーの謎解きをしてみましょう。
グループで話し合って謎を解き、英語で書いてみましょう。

<ちょっと一息>

ここでは、examples の *rhetoric*（例示による文章の展開）を練習してみましょう。トピック・センテンスをサポートするために、客観的・具体的な例を示すと、読者に書き手の主張がより効果的に伝わります。

Unit 7

Giving Examples

Exercise 1

次の各文のトピック・センテンスにふさわしい examples（具体例）を考えてみましょう。

1. Kyoto has many interesting places to visit.

a. _____

b. _____

2. Learning English can help you in many ways.

a. _____

b. _____

Exercise 2

次の英文を読んで下の問いに答えましょう。

Social Networking Services

　　Social networking services（SNS）are changing how people communicate. SNS ①（　　）Facebook and Snapchat allow people to share ideas, pictures, and videos. ②（　　）is Twitter; it is used to send short messages to many people at once. Other SNS ③（　　）Instagram and LINE are also popular ways to connect with friends. SNS are a powerful social tool.

1. トピック・センテンスに下線を引きましょう。

2.（　　）に下の（a）～（g）から適切な語句をいれましょう。答えは 1 つとは限りません。

> a）for instance　b）another example　c）like　d）an example　e）such as
> f）for example　g）a similar example

Exercise 3

"Life 100 Years Ago" というタイトルで、100 年前の人々の暮らしについて、例をあげて one paragraph で書いてみましょう。

Life 100 Years Ago

_____

_____

_____

_____

_____

Unit 8
The Case of the Lakeside Murder

Warm-up

cottage: 別荘のことです。他に villa, lodge, cabin などの言い方があります。cabin や lodge は cottage よりも素朴な作りで自然の中でキャンプをする時などに利用されます。villa は普通郊外や都市の良い場所にある別荘を言いますが、cottage は田舎にあって、小別荘と訳されることもあります。

master fuse: 家全体に流れる電流に使われているヒューズのことで、このスイッチを引くと家中の電気が消えます。ヒューズは一定以上の電流が流れて電気回路が加熱や発火するのを防止する電子部品です。

Key Vocabulary　語句の意味を下のリストから選びましょう。

1) confirm (　) 2) tilt (　) 3) instant (　) 4) play (v.) (　)
5) fetch (　) 6) directly (　) 7) wits (　) 8) quarter (　)
9) retire (　) 10) corpse (　)

a) 4分の1	b) 寝る、床につく	c) 知恵、五感	d) 直ちに
e) 連れてくる、来させる	f) (光が)差す	g) 瞬間、まさにそのとき	h) 確かめる
i) 死体	j) 傾く		

Vocabulary Exercise　Key Vocabulary の中から適当な語句を選びましょう。必要なら形を変えて完成文を訳しましょう。

1) A (　　) of an hour is fifteen minutes.

2) She used her (　　) when she was faced with an unexpected situation.

3) He (　　) his little child from the nearby park.

4) (　　) foods are bad for your health!

5) The deck (　　) quite suddenly.

Mystery Reading

"I need your opinion on the Topping murder," Sheriff Monahan said to Dr. Haledjian.

"Topping was the guest of Arthur Blair," began the sheriff. "The Blair cottage is about a quarter mile from mine on Lake Gentsch. Two nights ago, as I was retiring, I heard a shot from there.

"Hurrying outside, I met Blair running toward me. 'Come quickly!' he cried. 'Fritz Topping's been shot!'

"As we started for his place, Blair told me, 'Fritz and I were watching the late news on television when all of a sudden the lights went out. I started up to investigate when the front door swung open. A man with a rifle shot Fritz and disappeared before I could recover my wits.

"I saw Fritz had been shot in the heart and I ran directly to fetch you,' concluded Blair.

"The Blair cottage," the sheriff went on, "was dark. A little moonlight played in the living room where Fritz Topping sat in the chair. I had brought a flashlight and it took but an instant to confirm that he was dead.

"Somebody had pulled the master fuse in the garage. When we replaced it, the kitchen light and a table lamp behind the corpse went on. I could see the body was slightly tilted away from the front door.

"I told Blair to try to recall what he could."

The cottage was silent for a full minute before Blair shook his head. "I-it happened so fast. I've told you everything I can remember."

"Which," broke in Haledjian, "should be enough to bring him to trial for murder!"

(265 語)

WHY?

〈注〉
a quarter mile: 4分の1マイル　　**all of a sudden:** 急に、不意に
swing open: ドアをさっと開ける　　**recover one's wits:** 正気に戻る
break in: 口をはさむ、割り込む　　**bring a person to trial:** 公判に付する

34　　The Case of the Lakeside Murder

True or False

1) Dr. Haledjian was asked about the lakeside murder by Sheriff Monahan.　T/F
2) The Blair cottage was very near Dr. Haledjian's one.　T/F
3) Arthur Blair said he saw the man who shot Fritz with a rifle.　T/F
4) Fritz Topping and Arthur Blair were in the same house that night.　T/F
5) Fritz had pulled the master fuse in the living room just before the accident.　T/F

Comprehension Questions

1) Where was the Blair cottage located?
_____

2) What were Arthur and Fritz doing when the lights suddenly went out?
_____

Summary Dictation

Fritz Topping was ①(　　) at the house of Mr. Blair. As Blair told it, the two men had been watching TV when the power went out suddenly and an ②(　　) came in the front door and shot Topping. But when the ③(　　) arrived and restored power, the ④(　　) in Blair's story was brought to light, too. When the sheriff asked Haledjian to investigate, he quickly ⑤(　　) who the real killer was.

Mystery Solving

このミステリーの謎解きをしてみましょう。
グループで話し合って謎を解き、英語で書いてみましょう。

＜ちょっと一息＞

ここでは、 definition の *rhetoric* を練習してみましょう。Definition とは、ある言葉や表現がどういう意味かを説明する定義づけのことです。一つのパラグラフで definition を書く場合は、topic sentence で言葉や表現を定義づけます。次に、例（specific examples）などを書いて詳しく説明すると、分かりやすい文章が書けます。

Unit 8　35

Writing Definitions

Exercise 1

次の各文で、定義されている語句に下線を引きましょう。

1. Health can be defined as physical, mental and emotional well-being.
2. Computer graphics refers to the technology to generate images and designs on a computer screen.
3. Ethnomusicology is the study of music in its cultural context.

Exercise 2

英英辞書などを参考にして、（例）のように（　）に適語を入れ、英文を完成させましょう。

（例）Tennis is (a game) which is played by two people with racquets and a ball on a court.

1) A panda is （　　　） which/that_____

2) A doctor is （　　　） who/that_____

Exercise 3

Mystery Reading の中に出てくる "cottage" の definition を one paragraph で書いてみましょう。次の英文の続きを書いてください。

What Is a Cottage?

A cottage is a house that_____

_____

_____

_____

_____

_____

_____

_____

_____

_____

_____

The Case of the Lakeside Murder

Unit 9
The Case of the Hero Dog

Warm-up

five senses: 犬の五感について考えてみましょう。犬も人間同様に、五感（視覚、聴覚、嗅覚、味覚、触覚）を働かせて生活しています。特に嗅覚は、人間の100万倍で酢酸をかぎ分ける能力は1億倍だそうです。次に優れているのは聴覚で、人には聞こえない小さな音や高音も聞き取る能力を持っています。次は視覚ですが、犬には視神経の繊維数が人の1/5しかなく、視力は0.2〜0.3位だと言われています。しかし、暗い場所や、動いている物を見つける能力は人よりも優れています。さて、どのような世界が犬の眼前に広がっているのでしょうか。

Key Vocabulary　語句の意味を下のリストから選びましょう。

1) stony   (　) 2) disconsolately (　) 3) pitch   (　) 4) trip (*v.*) (　)
5) fabulous   (　) 6) clothesline   (　) 7) woeful (　) 8) wooer   (　)
9) canine   (　) 10) connoisseur   (　)

a) 口説き文句、宣伝文句	b) 悲惨な、嘆かわしい	c) 求婚者	d) イヌ（科の動物）
e) 専門家、目利き	f) 途方もない、すばらしい	g) わびしく、憂うつそうに	h) 石ころだらけの
i) つまずく	j) 物干し綱		

Vocabulary Exercise　Key Vocabularyの中から適当な語句を選びましょう。必要なら形を変えて完成文を訳しましょう。

1) Our family had a (　　　) experience during our summer vacation.
___

2) Tom (　　　) over a dog and fell down.
___

3) David tried to (　　　) the woman of his dreams.
___

4) My father hung the wash on the (　　　).
___

5) Judy was (　　　) about her husband's death.
___

Mystery Reading

"My pitch last night was beautiful." Cyril Makin, the woeful wooer, told Dr. Haledjian. "How did Trudy Shore ever see through it?

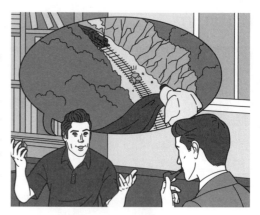

"For three generations," continued Makin, "Trudy's family have been circus people doing a dog act. If you aren't a canine connoisseur with a fabulous dog somewhere in the family, she won't date you twice. So to score with her, I made up a grandpa and his faithful four-legged helper."

Makin sipped his drink disconsolately. Then he recounted his latest unsuccessful pitch.

"Near Grandpa's farm the railroad tracks made a hairpin turn between two stony cliffs. From his fields, Grandpa could see the tracks. If rocks fell upon them, Grandpa climbed a hill and warned the engineer by waving a red flag.

"One day Grandpa saw rocks falling on the tracks. He started for the hill as a train approached, but tripped and knocked himself unconscious. That's when the dog proved his mettle.

"The dog raced to the house. The dog pulled down Grandpa's long red underwear from the clothesline, raced to the hill, and there ran back and forth, trailing the red underwear like a warning flag.

"The engineer saw the red signal and stopped the train, saving hundreds of passengers from death or injury!" concluded Makin.

"You're lucky," said Haledjian, "Trudy didn't bite your nose off for a dog story like that!"

(255 語)

WHAT WAS WRONG WITH IT?

〈注〉
see through: 〜を見通す、〜を看破する
score with: 〜を口説き落とす
act: (サーカスなどの) 出し物、演目
prove one's mettle: 気概 (やる気) を示す

True or False

1) Cyril Makin wanted to go on a date with Trudy Shore.　　　　　　　T/F
2) Trudy's family played with dogs in the theater.　　　　　　　　　　T/F
3) Cyril had a grandfather whose farm was on a large green field.　　　T/F
4) Cyril fell over the rocks and lost consciousness.　　　　　　　　　　T/F
5) Cyril said that finally the train stopped thanks to the red signal.　　T/F

Comprehension Questions

1) Why did Cyril Makin make up a story?
_____

2) In Cyril's story, what gave the dog a chance to become a hero?
_____

Summary Dictation

Cyril Makin tried to woo Trudy, a dog lover. He wanted to ①(　　　) to her that his family had a ②(　　　) dog so she would fall in love with him. He made up a story about his family's canine who ③(　　　) the day by signaling to the train engineer. ④(　　　), Trudy figured out his story was false, and Cyril was left to tell his tale disconsolately to Haledjian. But Haledjian was also not ⑤(　　　) with Cyril's story, as it contained a critical error.

Mystery Solving

このミステリーの謎解きをしてみましょう。
グループで話し合って謎を解き、英語で書いてみましょう。

<ちょっと一息>

ここでは、classificationの *rhetoric*（分類やグルーピングをすることにより展開する文章）の練習をします。classificationとは外観や性質をもとに分類することです。どのようなカテゴリーに分類したのかを明確にして、各グループを分かりやすく説明する練習をしてみましょう。

Classification

Exercise 1

次の単語をカテゴリーに分類し、下の表に記号で答えましょう。

a) ants	b) bees	c) cows	d) crocodiles	e) dragonflies	f) eagles	g) eels
h) frogs	i) horses	j) lions	k) newts	l) penguins	m) pigeons	n) red snappers
o) snakes	p) tunas	q) turtles

Classification type	Examples
Mammals	
Fish	
Birds	
Reptiles	
Insects	
Amphibians	

Exercise 2

次の英文を読んで、分類やグルーピングをしている語句に下線を引きましょう。

Television Programs

Television shows can be categorized into two major types: those based on a script ("scripted"), and those in which the script is not decided in advance ("unscripted"). Some examples of unscripted shows are: sporting events, game shows, reality shows, and interview programs. There are also many types of scripted shows such as documentaries, dramas, and variety shows. Further, within these television show subcategories there are additional sub-categories. For example, dramas may include, mystery dramas, historical dramas and romantic dramas.

Exercise 3

下の (a)〜(c) の中から1つ選び、Exercise 2のフォーマットを参考にして classification の *rhetoric* を使って one paragraph で書いてみましょう。

a) music　　b) movies　　c) books

40　　The Case of the Hero Dog

Unit 10
The Case of the Million-to-One Shot

Warm-up

duel: 決闘、果たし合いのことです。原則として1対1で事前に決められた同一の条件のもと、武器を持って生命を賭して戦い、勝負を決めます。ヨーロッパでは、紛争を格闘によって解決したゲルマン民族の風習が起源とされ、6世紀には制度として存在していました。武器として最初は棍棒と盾、中世では剣、フランス革命後は銃が使われました。アメリカでも、開拓時代にしばしば行われ、日本では1612年の宮本武蔵と佐々木小次郎による巌流島での決闘が有名です。現在では、ほとんどの国で法的に禁止されています。

Key Vocabulary　語句の意味を下のリストから選びましょう。

1) marksman (　) 2) simultaneously (　) 3) mystic (　) 4) phenomenon (　)
5) duel (　) 6) damsel (　) 7) extraordinary (　) 8) repute (*v.*) (　)
9) resign (　) 10) wildest (　)

a) 並外れた	b) 現象	c) とてつもない	d) 辞める、断念する
e) 決闘	f) 評する、見なす	g) 射撃の名手	h) 女の子、乙女
i) 同時に	j) 神秘的な		

Vocabulary Exercise　Key Vocabulary の中から適当な語句を選びましょう。必要なら形を変えて完成文を訳しましょう。

1) Due to ill health, she (　　) as a Diet member.
___

2) My (　　) dream has come true.
___

3) Dr. Brown is (　　) to be the best cardiac surgeon in Canada.
___

4) Even a poor (　　) will hit the target with enough shots.
___

5) A rainbow is a natural (　　).
___

Mystery Reading

"The law of averages will sooner or later produce an extraordinary event," said Dr. Haledjian. "If taken by itself, such an event appears as a phenomenon—the product of wildest chance. Actually, it is but a logical variation from the common mass of nearly similar events."

Haledjian paused to hand Octavia a cup of coffee.

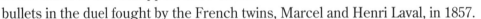

Then he resumed. "An excellent illustration is the disappearance of the bullets in the duel fought by the French twins, Marcel and Henri Laval, in 1857.

"Except that Marcel was left-handed, the twins were so alike that even their parents had difficulty telling them apart.

"Henri and Marcel received excellent military educations, and were soon reputed the best marksmen in the French Army. Inevitably, they fell in love with the same damsel. For young men of honor, one solution only was possible. A duel.

"You may picture it now, after a hundred years. The brothers standing back to back as had hundreds before them; then marching and wheeling at the count like mirror images.

"They fired simultaneously. To the second, the shots sounded as one. By a miracle, the brothers weren't scratched, though both confessed to having aimed to kill.

"The pistols were examined and found in perfect working order. Yet neither in the barn behind Marcel, nor the fence behind Henri, was either bullet located.

"The disappearance of the bullets into thin air had a mystic effect on the twins. They resigned their commissions. As the object of the duel ran off with a Hungarian nobleman, they married twin sisters of a merchant of Marseille.

"Now I've given you the clues—the law of averages and the similarity of the twins, Octavia, my dear," concluded Haledjian. "You should have no trouble in determining what really happened to the two bullets."

(296 語)

WHAT?

〈注〉
million to one:（可能性などが）極めて低い　　**sooner or later:** いつかは、遅かれ早かれ
wildest chance: 全くの偶然

The Case of the Million-to-One Shot

True or False

1) Dr. Haledjian drank a cup of coffee handed to him by Octavia. T/F
2) Marcel and Henri Laval were born in 1857 in France. T/F
3) One of the twins was left-handed. T/F
4) The bullets were found in the barn behind Marcel and the fence behind Henri. T/F
5) The damsel who was the reason for the duel married a Hungarian nobleman. T/F

Comprehension Questions

1) What kind of education did Marcel and Henri receive?

2) Who did the twins marry in the end?

Summary Dictation

Dr. Haledjian tells the amazing story of twin brothers who fight each other in a ①(   ). The twins are ②(   ) except one is right-handed, and the other is left-handed. Both are ③(   ) marksmen. At the time of the duel, only one shot is heard, and ④(   ) brother is injured. Why? What happened to the ⑤(   ) in this bizarre story? In the end, neither brother won the duel. Did the law of averages produce an extraordinary event?

Mystery Solving

このミステリーの謎解きをしてみましょう。
グループで話し合って謎を解き、英語で書いてみましょう。

＜ちょっと一息＞

ここでは、 comparison の *rhetoric* （類似点を挙げて展開する文章）を練習してみましょう。二つのものを比較して、その共通点を説明するものを comparison といいます。たとえば、2人の人物は比較できますが、1人の人物とある民族全体を比較することはできません。次に同じ基準で比較することです。たとえば、一方を「身長」で他方を「体重」でというように違う基準で比較することはできません。Unit 10 は比較（類似点）に焦点を合わせて述べる練習です。

Comparison

Exercise 1
(　　) 内の語を使って英文をつなげましょう。

1. Tea is a drink. Coffee is a drink.（both）
_____

2. Time is limited. Money is limited.（the same as）
_____

3. Humans are mammals. Whales are mammals.（like）
_____

Exercise 2
ここでは類似点に焦点を当てて述べる練習です。【ヒント】を参考にして、**"Tokyo and London"** というタイトルで、下の英文の続きを書いてみましょう。

【ヒント】（すべて使わなくてもいいです）
capital, location, royal family, seasons, attractions, transportation

Tokyo and London

トピック・センテンス	Tokyo and London have many things in common.
サポーティング・センテンス	First, _____
サポーティング・センテンス	_____
サポーティング・センテンス	_____
コンクルーディング・センテンス	It is clear that both of these two cities _____

Exercise 3

"Tokyo Disneyland and Universal Studios Japan" というタイトルで comparison（類似点）の *rhetoric* を使って one paragraph で書いてみましょう。

Tokyo Disneyland and Universal Studios Japan

_____
_____
_____
_____

Review Test 2: Unit 6〜Unit 10

▶ I *Photographs*

1. (A)   (B)   (C)   (D)

2. (A)   (B)   (C)   (D)

3. (A)   (B)   (C)   (D)

4. (A)   (B)   (C)   (D)

▶ II *Question-Response*

1) Mark your answer on your answer sheet.   (A)   (B)   (C)
2) Mark your answer on your answer sheet.   (A)   (B)   (C)
3) Mark your answer on your answer sheet.   (A)   (B)   (C)
4) Mark your answer on your answer sheet.   (A)   (B)   (C)
5) Mark your answer on your answer sheet.   (A)   (B)   (C)

▶ III 文法・語彙

1. David was walking through the park (　　　) his hands in his pockets.
   A) for B) by C) with D) besides

2. Recently our company does not allow any employees (　　) overtime beyond 9 pm.
   A) work B) working C) will work D) to work

3. The heavy snow prevented John from (　　) to the meeting on time.
   A) come B) to come C) came D) coming

4. The baseball team owners' financial crunch will get even (　　　) next season because their TV revenues could drop by half.
   A) bad B) as bad as C) worse D) worst

5. For (　　) wish to be involved in the planning of the school festival, there is a meeting on Saturday at 6 pm.
   A) whose B) whom C) those who D) whoever

6. Everyone in the classroom waited for Mary to speak, but she remained (　　　).
   A) silence B) silent C) silently D) silences

7. (　　) she fastened her safety belt, she would not have been killed.
   A) Just B) As C) Had D) Although

8. (　　) you weren't at the meeting last night?
   A) Why B) How come C) How many D) How about

9. According to the guidebook, this white castle (　　) about 1000 years ago.
   A) is said to be built B) was said to be built
   C) is said to have been built D) is said to have built

10. We all neither confirm (　　) deny the existence of this organization.
    A) and B) or C) nor D) while

46

Unit 11
The Case of the Missing Button

Warm-up

grade: アメリカでは学年を grade で呼びます。アメリカの学校制度は地域によって異なります。一般的には elementary school（小学校）は first grade（1年）から fifth grade（5年）まで、middle school（中学校）は小6から中2、high school（高校）は中3から高3までです。この物語に登場する Matty は tenth-grade student（10年生）なので日本の高校1年生になります。

Key Vocabulary　語句の意味を下のリストから選びましょう。

1) husky　（　）　2) nut　（　）　3) slug　（　）　4) corridor　（　）
5) demand　（　）　6) spot　（　）　7) clasp　（　）　8) retort　（　）
9) positive　（　）　10) silly　（　）

a) ばか者	b) 詰問する	c) 見つける、見分ける	d) がっしりした
e) 確信している	f) 握りしめる	g) 言い返す	h) 殴る
i) ばかげた	j) 廊下		

Vocabulary Exercise　Key Vocabulary の中から適当な語句を選びましょう。必要なら形を変えて完成文を訳しましょう。

1) She was scared of the dim school (　　　).

2) I am (　　　) that he will come to the party tomorrow.

3) How (　　　) of you to do such a thing!

4) She was (　　　) early in the morning in the snow.

5) "I will not do overtime," she (　　　).

Unit 11　47

Mystery Reading

Matty Linden, a husky tenth-grade student, scowled at Inspector Winters. "You must be some kind of nut. I didn't slug Miss Casey, and I didn't steal her purse!"

"No? Unfortunately for you, a ninth-grade girl happened to enter the corridor where Miss Casey lay. The girl saw a boy in a dark cardigan sweater and brown pants leaving by the door at the far end."

The inspector paused and then demanded, "Do you always wear your sweater buttoned?"

"Sure," replied Matty. "Why?"

"Because you might have noticed the third button from the top is missing," snapped the inspector. He held up the missing button. "The girl who spotted you found the button clasped in Miss Casey's hand."

"I lost that button two days ago," retorted Matty. "This girl—how could she be sure it was me in that long corridor?"

"She isn't positive—she saw only your back. But this missing button proves you did it. Luckily, Miss Casey isn't badly hurt. Now, where's her purse?"

"Matty kept insisting he didn't know a thing about the slugging and theft," the inspector told Dr. Haledjian later.

"No doubt," said Haledjian, "the boy had some silly alibi about where he was when Miss Casey was slugged and robbed?"

"Right. He claims he got a note to be in the school boiler room at ten—fifteen minutes before Miss Casey was assaulted. He waited half an hour, but nobody showed up."

"I trust you made an arrest?" asked Haledjian.

(252 語)

WHAT WAS THE GUILTY STUDENT'S ERROR?

〈注〉
scowl: にらみつける **button:** ボタンで閉じる
snap: 鋭い口調で言う **assault:** 襲撃する

True or False

1) Matty Linden looked strong and powerful.　　　　　　　　　　　　　　T/F
2) Unfortunately, Miss Casey was found dead.　　　　　　　　　　　　　　T/F
3) At first, Inspector Winters believed what the girl said.　　　　　　　　T/F
4) The girl who said that she had seen a boy was younger than Matty Linden.　T/F
5) Inspector Winters asked Dr. Haledjian to help him solve the case.　　　T/F

Comprehension Questions

1) Where was Miss Casey found?
___

2) Where was Matty Linden's cardigan button?
___

Summary Dictation

Miss Casey was attacked and her purse was stolen. She had a button in her hand which Matty said he had ①(　　　). Moreover, a girl said that she saw a boy from the back at a ②(　　　) near the scene of the ③(　　　) and that he wore a cardigan. Inspector Winters was ④(　　　) of Matty. However, Matty insisted that he was in the school boiler room when Miss Casey was attacked. What was ⑤(　　　) with what the guilty student said?

Mystery Solving

このミステリーの謎解きをしてみましょう。
グループで話し合って謎を解き、英語で書いてみましょう。

<ちょっと一息>

ここでは、 contrast の *rhetoric* （相違点による展開）について練習してみましょう。contrast は二つのものを対比させて相違点を説明するものです。ここでは対比（相違点）に焦点を合わせて述べる練習をします。

Unit 11　　49

Contrast

Exercise 1
下の語句から適語を選び（　　　）に入れなさい。文頭にくる語も小文字にしてあります。
1. Using trains costs (　　) than using cars in a big city.
2. The climates in Tokyo and that in Sapporo are (　　).
3. Mike is a lazy student. (　　), Sam is hardworking.
4. (　　) she eats a lot of cake, she stays slim.

on the other hand	although	less	different

Exercise 2
次の語句を正しく並べ替えましょう。相違を表す語句に○をつけましょう。文頭にくる語も小文字にしてあります

1. Tokyo Sky Tree / Tokyo Tower / the new / from / is / the old / different

_____

2. tea / unlike / has / coffee / caffeine / less

_____

3. however, / more / tea / coffee / antioxidants / has / than

_____

Exercise 3
下の絵を見て、contrast（相違点）の *rhetoric* を使って、二人の人物の相違点を書いてみましょう。

Mike and Chris

Mike

Chris

50　　The Case of the Missing Button

Unit 12
The Case of the Gold Brick

Warm-up

gold brick: 金の延べ棒ことです。gold bar, gold bullion, gold ingot とも言います。山吹色の輝く金は世界中で古くから私たちを魅了してきました。その理由の一つは希少性で、これまでに採掘された総量はオリンピック規定のプール3杯分しかありません。金はとても柔らかいので、1gで3000mの線にまで伸ばすことができます。また見た目よりずっと重く（同じ体積で水の19.34倍）、手のひらに乗るぐらいの延べ棒が1kgです。

Key Vocabulary　語句の意味を下のリストから選びましょう。

1) pan (v.)　(　)　2) sly　(　)　3) prospector　(　)　4) contract　(　)
5) expedition　(　)　6) bonanza　(　)　7) provisions　(　)　8) salvage　(　)
9) ingeniously　(　)　10) reproachfully　(　)

a) 大もうけ	b) 器用に	c) 契約（書）	d) 食料
e) 救い出す	f) 選鉱鍋で採取する	g) 探検（隊）	h) 探鉱者
i) 非難がましく	j) ずるい、いたずらな		

Vocabulary Exercise　Key Vocabulary の中から適当な語句を選びましょう。必要なら形を変えて完成文を訳しましょう。

1) A (　　　) person is good at using others.

2) It is important to have (　　　) for natural disasters.

3) The teacher often points out my mistakes (　　　).

4) Our class went on a geological (　　　) to learn about different kinds of rocks.

5) The coins were (　　　) from the sunken ship.

Mystery Reading

"My great-grandfather, Everet Lamont Sydney, panned gold from a secret stream and by 1875 was the richest man in California," said Mrs. Sydney, a sly twinkle in her eye.

"On his death bed, he told two old prospectors, Jepp Hanson and Oscar Tyre, the way to the stream and agreed to let them pan for gold, provided they swore never to divulge the location or make more than one trip themselves.

"Jepp and Oscar signed a contract, which stated: 'Whatever gold Jepp Hanson and Oscar Tyre or any individual in their expedition can carry by himself from the stream to the home of Everet Sydney shall be given to said individual.'

"Naturally, Jepp and Oscar didn't bring anyone else in on their bonanza. They set out by themselves the next morning, having loaded Jepp's old mule with enough tools and provisions to stay in the wilds six months.

"They had hardly got to the stream when a landslide buried their equipment. All the two prospectors salvaged were the shorts they wore at night, the mule, and two pans.

"Since the contract said they could make only one trip, they stayed on, living off wild berries and nuts. After five months they got enough gold dust, which, to prevent being blown, they ingeniously melted into a brick. That small brick, measuring but a foot long, six inches wide, and six inches high, would make them millionaires.

"My great-grandfather died while they were away, and the two old-timers took their case to court. Each insisted he had been the one who carried the brick.

"The judge peered at the brick and at the contract, and awarded the gold—to whom?"

Dr. Haledjian shook his head reproachfully. "My dear Mrs. Sydney. You are forever trying to trip up an old sleuth."

And so that the other guests couldn't hear, he whispered, "To—"

(307 語)

TO WHOM?

〈注〉
said: 上述の　　　mule: ラバ　　　live off: 〜だけを食べて生きる
old-timer: 老人　　　trip up: やりこめる

52　The Case of the Gold Brick

True or False

1) Nobody but Everet Sydney knew the location of the stream. T/F
2) Both Jepp and Oscar were allowed to keep all the gold they found. T/F
3) Jepp and Oscar took someone with them to help. T/F
4) A landslide happened just after they got to the stream. T/F
5) Jepp and Oscar ate berries and nuts besides the food they brought. T/F

Comprehension Questions

1) How did Everet Lamont Sydney become the richest man in California?
   _____

2) What are the two conditions Everet Lamont Sydney gave to the two prospectors?
   _____

Summary Dictation

Everet allowed Jepp and Oscar to pan for gold at a ①(　　) and said the one who carried the ②(　　) back to his house could have the gold. They left for the stream with a ③(　　), tools and provisions. They melted the gold dust they gathered into a ④(　　), which was one foot long, six inches ⑤(　　), and six inches high. On the way back, each insisted that they were the one who deserved the brick. Who deserved the brick the most?

Mystery Solving

このミステリーの謎解きをしてみましょう。
グループで話し合って謎を解き、英語で書いてみましょう。

＜ちょっと一息＞

ここでは、cause and effect の *rhetoric*（因果関係を論理的に説明するタイプの文章）を練習してみましょう。手法は、結果を述べることから始めその原因を列挙し、説明しながら進める場合と、最初に原因を挙げ、その結果とともに結論づける場合の2種類があります。

Describing Cause and Effect

Exercise 1

(a)〜(g) から適語を選び、(　　　) に書き入れて文を完成しましょう。必要なら形を変えてください。

a) as a result	b) because	c) cause	d) consequently
e) contribute to	f) result in	g) since	

1. (　　　) that bakery's cake is so delicious, there is always a long line.
2. The flood (　　　) a lot of damage.
3. Her plan (　　　) a huge success for the company.
4. I studied hard before the test and (　　　), I got the best mark in the class.

Exercise 2

下の文章を指示に従って書き換えましょう。

1. My professor had influenza so she had to cancel classes.
   （例）cause を使って　My professor's influenza caused her to cancel classes.
   a) due to を使って＿＿＿＿＿＿＿＿＿＿＿＿＿＿＿＿＿＿＿＿＿＿＿＿
   b) result in を使って＿＿＿＿＿＿＿＿＿＿＿＿＿＿＿＿＿＿＿＿＿＿
2. It was raining so the picnic was postponed until next Sunday.
   a) since を使って＿＿＿＿＿＿＿＿＿＿＿＿＿＿＿＿＿＿＿＿＿＿＿＿
   b) consequently を使って＿＿＿＿＿＿＿＿＿＿＿＿＿＿＿＿＿＿＿

Exercise 3

下の絵を見て、cause and effect（因果関係）の *rhetoric* を用いて **"Why Is Tom Not Healthy"** というタイトルで書いてみましょう。

Why Is Tom Not Healthy

＿＿＿＿＿＿＿＿＿＿＿＿＿＿＿＿＿＿＿＿＿＿＿＿＿＿＿＿＿＿＿＿＿＿＿＿＿＿
＿＿＿＿＿＿＿＿＿＿＿＿＿＿＿＿＿＿＿＿＿＿＿＿＿＿＿＿＿＿＿＿＿＿＿＿＿＿
＿＿＿＿＿＿＿＿＿＿＿＿＿＿＿＿＿＿＿＿＿＿＿＿＿＿＿＿＿＿＿＿＿＿＿＿＿＿
＿＿＿＿＿＿＿＿＿＿＿＿＿＿＿＿＿＿＿＿＿＿＿＿＿＿＿＿＿＿＿＿＿＿＿＿＿＿

Unit 13
The Case of the Dying Brazilian

Warm-up

Brazil: 南アメリカ最大の面積を持つ国です。リオデジャネイロで毎年行われるリオのカーニバルは世界で一番有名なお祭りと言われています。ブラジルはまた日本と深い繋がりのある国で、1908年に日本人が初めて移民として渡り、それ以来ブラジルの発展に大いに貢献しています。

Key Vocabulary　語句の意味を下のリストから選びましょう。

1) phony (   )　2) tip (   )　3) informer (   )　4) kidnap (   )
5) confide (   )　6) ransom (   )　7) freighter (   )　8) bundle (   )
9) growl (   )　10) interpret (   )

a) 唸る	b) 貨物船	c) 大金	d) 通訳する
e) にせの	f) 秘密情報	g) 秘密を打ち明ける	h) 密告者
i) 身代金	j) 誘拐する		

Vocabulary Exercise　Key Vocabulary の中から適当な語句を選びましょう。必要なら形を変えて完成文を訳しましょう。

1) They (   ) the girl and demanded a ransom.
_____

2) He (   ) in his wife about the plot to kidnap the girl, leading to his arrest.
_____

3) The patient got worse after taking the herb she got from the (   ) doctor.
_____

4) She works as an (   ) at international conferences.
_____

5) The informer's (   ) helped the police find the man.
_____

Unit 13　55

Mystery Reading

It had been months since Nick the Nose had slipped into Inspector Winters' office to peddle a phony tip.

"I got something on the Nilo Bernardes case," the greasy little informer confided slyly.

"Nilo Bernardes," Nick explained to Haledjian, "is a 10-year-old boy who was kidnapped last month in Santos, Brazil. His father, a millionaire, paid the ransom. The boy has not been returned."

"Last night," said Nick, "this old guy in Pedro's flop started to talk as he lay dying. At first he ran on about how he had lived all his life in Brazil and never did anything wrong till last month. Then he got interesting.

"He said he had sinned by collecting the ransom money for young Nilo. Before he got paid his share, he had overheard the rest of the kidnap gang plotting to kill him.

"So that night he stowed away on a freighter and jumped ship in America. With his dying breath, he named the town in Brazil where the kidnappers were laying low.

"Of course, he spoke in Spanish and I didn't understand him. But Pedro, who is Mexican, understood and did the interpreting. Pedro will back me up.

"I figure," concluded Nick, "that the name of the town where the kidnappers are hiding is worth a bundle!"

The inspector rose, growling. Haledjian barely had time to open the office door before Nick went sailing out.

(233 語)

WHY WAS NICK GIVEN THE HEAVE-HO?

〈注〉
peddle: 売る
stow away: 密航する
lie low: 身を隠す
run on: 話し続ける
jump ship: 一目散に逃げる
heave-ho: 追い出すこと

True or False

1) Nick is an inspector. T/F
2) The kidnapped boy was released after his father paid the ransom. T/F
3) Pedro's flop is in Brazil. T/F
4) The old guy didn't want the kidnappers to kill the boy. T/F
5) Nick said that Pedro helped him get information from the old guy. T/F

Comprehension Questions

1) Why did the old guy in Pedro's Flop say that he escaped?
___
2) Who did Nick say could support his story?
___

Summary Dictation

Nick came to Inspector Winters' office to inform him of an old man involved in a 10-year-old boy's ①(   ). Nick met him at Pedro's flop. The old man was in charge of collecting the ②(   ) for the boy. Learning he would be ③(   ) after handing over the money, he fled. He told the story to Nick in Spanish. Nick didn't understand ④(   ), so Pedro ⑤(   ) it for him. After listening to the ridiculous story, Winters threw Nick out.

Mystery Solving

このミステリーの謎解きをしてみましょう。
グループで話し合って謎を解き、英語で書いてみましょう。

＜ちょっと一息＞

ここでは、from a paragraph to an essay の段階に進みます。エッセイとは「自分の意見を自由な形式で、気のむくままに表現した散文や随筆」ではなく、「自分の意見を論理的、分析的に説明したもの」で、いわゆる小論文のことです。エッセイは Introduction（序論）–Body（本論）–Conclusion（結論）の3つの部分で構成されています。英語でレポートなどのエッセイを書く場合、どのような点に注意すればいいのか、しっかりと学びましょう。

Developing Paragraphs into Essays

Exercise 1

ここではパラグラフからエッセイへの展開の仕方について学びましょう。

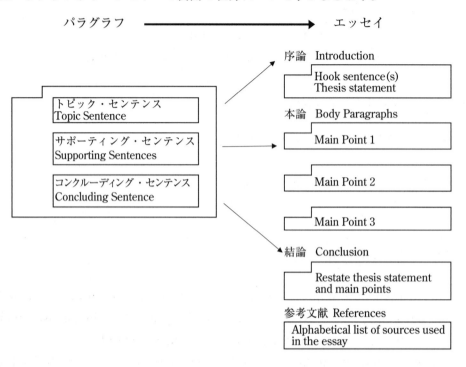

Exercise 2

"**Spring in Japan**" についての英文を読み、5パラグラフのエッセイの型に従って並べ替えて、上の図に番号を入れましょう。

Spring in Japan

①   First, many gorgeous flowers bloom in the spring. The season begins when plum trees bloom with a deep pink color. Then sakura cherry trees dazzle everyone with their light pink display. Other flowers such as tulips and azaleas also add to the seasonal beauty. Springtime is full of color.

②   Spring is a lively season in Japan. Flowers bloom to make beautiful scenery. Festivals encourage people to enjoy going out after the long winter. And a variety of contemporary events also entertain many people. There are many things to see and do in spring in Japan.

③   Finally, people can also enjoy a variety of modern events. Fans of anime look forward to the Tokyo Anime Fair. Sake tours in Kyoto delight enthusiasts. And the Okinawa Film Festival offers the latest in Japanese and Asian films.

④   Cherry blossom viewing parties may be popular, but there are many more things to see and do in Japan in the spring. From enjoying the flowers to attending a variety of events, Japan has plenty of things to do in this wonderful season.

⑤   In addition, the warm weather brings a season of traditional festivals. The Takayama Festival in Gifu prefecture is held in April. In addition, the Aoi Matsuri in Kyoto takes place in May. Visitors can enjoy parades, dances and traditional food at these events.

Exercise 3

"My Favorite Season" というタイトルで、Introduction-Body-Conclusion で構成されたエッセイを書いてみましょう。

My Favorite Season

_____

_____

_____

_____

_____

_____

_____

_____

_____

_____

_____

_____

_____

_____

_____

_____

_____

_____

_____

[MEMO]

Unit 14
The Case of the Stranded Blonde

Warm-up

Albany: アメリカ合衆国ニューヨーク州の州都です。ハドソン川の西岸、ニューヨーク市の北、約 240km に位置します。昔から交通の要衝となっています。

martini: カクテルの一種で、ジンとベルモットを合わせオリーブを飾ります。「カクテルはマティーニに始まりマティーニで終わる」と言われるほど奥深い飲み物で「カクテルの王様」と呼ばれています。レシピは約 250 種類以上あります。

Key Vocabulary　語句の意味を下のリストから選びましょう。

1) related　　　(　)　2) overtake　(　)　3) endeavor　(　)　4) embarrassment (　)
5) utter　　　 (　)　6) bellow　　(　)　7) blunder　　(　)　8) plot　　　　　(　)
9) conspirator (　)　10) alert　　(　)

a) 誤り	b) 共謀者	c) 〜しようと努める	d) たくらみ
e) 当惑	f) 述べる	g) 発する	h) 降りかかる
i) 用心深い	j) どなる		

Vocabulary Exercise　Key Vocabulary の中から適当な語句を選びましょう。必要なら形を変えて完成文を訳しましょう。

1) We'll (　　　) to satisfy our customers.

2) He made a (　　　) on the project and was removed from the position.

3) It's important to stay (　　　) when visiting a new city.

4) I was so surprised that I couldn't (　　　) a word.

5) I was (　　　) by sadness when I heard about his death.

Unit 14　　61

Mystery Reading

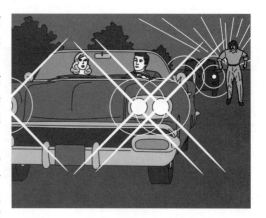

A look of satisfaction settled on young Harrington's face as he sat at dinner with Dr. Haledjian.

"Last week I put to good use my long association with you, Doctor." The handsome youth puffed a moment on his cigar. Then he related what had happened to him.

"I was driving my convertible up to Albany when night overtook me, still fifty miles from my destination. I thought I'd better double check my route, and so I inquired at a roadside tavern.

"While I was endeavoring to catch the bartender's eye, an extraordinarily beautiful woman sat down on the stool next to mine.

"She begged my forgiveness for speaking, and, quite covered with embarrassment, confessed she had left her purse on the bus. What could I do?

"After three rounds of martinis, she refused another drink, but demurely asked for a quarter for the bus home. 'Nonsense!' I protested and escorted her to my car.

"We had driven but a mile when a pair of headlights swung into the road behind me. The girl turned around and uttered a cry. 'My husband! He'll kill us both!'

"The road being dark and unfamiliar, I decided against a race. I pulled to the side and stopped. So did the black sedan following us. An enormous man jumped out, bellowing wrathfully. But I put an end to his posturing by pointing out the blunder in their plot. I drove off, leaving the pair of conspirators furious but far wiser."

"Congratulations," said Haledjian. "A simple case, but an instructive one. Henceforth you will be alert to the cunning behind a pretty face."

(267 語)

HOW DID HARRINGTON KNOW HE WAS BEING FRAMED?

〈注〉
put ～ to good use: ～を有効に使う　**round:** ひとわたり分（の飲み物）
demurely: 控え目に　**wrathfully:** 激怒して
put an end to ~: ～を終わらせる　**henceforth:** これからは

62　The Case of the Stranded Blonde

True or False

1) As soon as Harrington entered the tavern, he ordered a drink. T/F
2) The woman asked Harrington for a drink. T/F
3) Harrington thought it was nonsense to give her a ride. T/F
4) Harrington decided not to race against the black sedan. T/F
5) A pair of headlights approached Harrington's car when he drove 50 miles. T/F

Comprehension Questions

1) Who was involved in this case?

2) Where was Harrington supposed to take the woman after drinking?

Summary Dictation

One night, Harrington dropped by a ①(   ). A blonde woman came and asked for a ②(   ) for the bus home because she'd left her purse on the bus. He offered her a ride home. They drove about a mile when they noticed a pair of ③(   ) behind them. Seeing them, the woman cried, "It's my ④(   )! He'll kill us!" Harrington stopped his car, pointed out the error in their ⑤(   ) to the woman and her furious husband, and drove off.

Mystery Solving

このミステリーの謎解きをしてみましょう。
グループで話し合って謎を解き、英語で書いてみましょう。

<ちょっと一息>

ここでも、essay を書く練習をします。まずパラグラフから essay への展開についての理解を深めましょう。複数のパラグラフを繋ぎ合わせてより内容の深いエッセイを作成するためには、書く前にエッセイ全体の構成をよく考えることが大切です。実際にインターネットを参照しながらエッセイを書いてみましょう。

Writing an Essay: Using Internet Resources

Exercise 1
"**Japanese Culture**" のタイトルでエッセイを書いてみましょう。必要な情報をインターネットで検索して収集します。引用した URL は必ず明記しておきましょう。

URL:

Exercise 2
Appendix 2 を参考にして、アウトラインを英語で作成してみましょう。
1）Introduction
2）Body: Main Point 1
3）Body: Main Point 2
4）Body: Main Point 3
5）Conclusion

Exercise 3
次に Introduction-Body-Conclusion からなる 3 ～ 5 パラグラフのエッセイを書いてみましょう。

Japanese Culture

_____

_____

_____

_____

_____

_____

_____

_____

_____

_____

_____

_____

Unit 15
The Case of the Purse Snatcher

Warm-up

pocketbook: 女性用の肩ひものない小型のハンドバッグのことで，purse ともいいます。
fire exit: 非常口のことです。Emergency exit ともいい、非常時の際の命を守る大事なドアです。その仕様は消防法で細かく定められています。

Key Vocabulary 語句の意味を下のリストから選びましょう。

1) petty (　)　2) questioning (　)　3) charge (*n.*) (　)　4) snatch (　)
5) wail (　)　6) duck (*v.*) (　)　7) alley (　)　8) innocent (　)
9) chuck (　)　10) usher (　)

a) 急いで隠れる	b) つまらない	c) 罪、告訴	d) 泣き叫ぶ
e) 投げる	f) ひったくる	g) 無実の	h) 誘導する
i) 路地	j) 尋問		

Vocabulary Exercise　Key Vocabulary の中から適当な語句を選びましょう。必要なら形を変えて完成文を訳しましょう。

1) The man (　　　) behind the tree when she looked back.

2) The police made a (　　　) of conspiracy against the couple.

3) The secretary (　　　) me into the president's office for a job interview.

4) I am tired of listening to customers' (　　　) complaints.

5) Her room is very messy with the clothes she has (　　　) everywhere.

Mystery Reading

Dr. Haledjian was in Inspector Winters' office when Bumbles Brasoon, the nation's most inexpert petty crook, was brought in for questioning.

"The charge is purse snatching outside the new theater on Washington Avenue," snapped the inspector.

"It's a case of mistaken identity!" wailed Bumbles.

"The complainant, Mrs. Ruth Fogerty, didn't give you her pocketbook, now did she?" chided the inspector.

"No, but the real crook did," said Bumbles. "I'll tell you what happened, and it's the truth. I swear on my wife's honor!

"I was walking past the theater thinking about looking for a job when the weather improves. Suddenly I hear a woman scream. This big kid with long hair comes hot-footing past me, carrying a pocketbook.

"He ducks into the alley behind the theater. I give chase like a good citizen. He gets to the theater's fire exit door when he spots me.

"He knows I've got him. So he chucks me the pocketbook, pushes open the door, and slips inside. I'm holding the pocketbook when this rhino of a dame comes charging up the alley with a cop," concluded Bumbles. "I'm innocent!"

After Bumbles had been ushered out, the inspector said to Haledjian, "Mrs. Fogerty isn't certain who snatched her pocketbook. Bumbles' story is weak, but it might be true."

"His story is impossible," said Haledjian.

(219 語)

WHY?

〈注〉
mistaken identity: 人違い **complainant:** 原告
chide: たしなめる **hot-foot:** 大急ぎで行く
give chase: 追跡する **this rhino of a dame:** 金持ちの老婦人

66   The Case of the Purse Snatcher

True or False

1) Bumbles was jobless. T/F
2) Bumbles said that a man with a pocketbook in his hand walked past him. T/F
3) Bumbles said that the exit was left open when the young man spotted him. T/F
4) A policeman saw Bumbles holding a pocketbook in front of the theater. T/F
5) Mrs. Fogerty didn't see the snatcher's face. T/F

Comprehension Questions

1) On what charge was Bumbles arrested?
___
2) According to Bumbles, where did the real culprit see Bumbles?
___

Summary Dictation

The police arrested Bumbles for purse ①(　　　) He argued he was innocent. He said he saw a young man run past him with a ②(　　　) after hearing a woman's cry. He chased the man into the ③(　　　) behind the theater. As soon as the man saw him, he threw the pocketbook at him, ④(　　　) the exit door open and slipped inside. Haledjian could quickly tell that Bumbles was telling a ⑤(　　　).

Mystery Solving

このミステリーの謎解きをしてみましょう。
グループで話し合って謎を解き、英語で書いてみましょう。

<ちょっと一息>

ここでは論理的で説得力のある argumentative essay （論証文）を書く練習をしてみましょう。これは今まで練習してきたような単に物事を客観的に説明するだけの文章ではなく、賛成か反対かなどの価値判断を下して、自分の意見の正しさを明確に示し、それを主張するものです。以下の点に注意しましょう。1) 自分の意見や立場を明確にして書く。2) 読者を強く意識して書く（たとえば自分とは反対の意見を持っていると想定する）。3) 自分の意見や立場を、書いている途中で絶対に変えない（論理的に首尾一貫させる）。

Writing an Argumentative Essay

Exercise 1

Counter-arguments（反論）の書きかたを学びましょう。下のヒントを参考にして反論を書きましょう。

（例）Mobile phones should be banned in classrooms

<u>Although</u> mobile phones are often banned in classrooms, <u>sometimes</u> they are useful.

1. Autumn is the best season in Japan._____

_____

2. Exercise is healthy. _____

_____

【ヒント】

Although	While	However	It may be true that	Despite

Exercise 2

"Living in a Big City" について、以下に賛成・反対の両方の欄に意見を書いてみましょう。

For（賛成）	Against（反対）

Exercise 3

Exercise 2 の表をもとに Introduction-Body-Conclusion の構成でエッセイを書きましょう。Body の 1 つに against を入れてみましょう。

Living in a Big City

（例）

Introduction
Body: Main Point 1
Body: Main Point 2
Body: Main Point 3
Conclusion

Review Test 3: Unit 11～Unit 15

▶ I Photographs

1. (A)   (B)   (C)   (D)
2. (A)   (B)   (C)   (D)
3. (A)   (B)   (C)   (D)
4. (A)   (B)   (C)   (D)

▶ II Question-Response

1) Mark your answer on your answer sheet.   (A)   (B)   (C)
2) Mark your answer on your answer sheet.   (A)   (B)   (C)
3) Mark your answer on your answer sheet.   (A)   (B)   (C)
4) Mark your answer on your answer sheet.   (A)   (B)   (C)
5) Mark your answer on your answer sheet.   (A)   (B)   (C)

▶ III 文法・語彙

1. I had (　　) left home when I felt the earth shake.
   A) sooner   B) hardly   C) later   D) ever

2. (　　) that you give me your address, I can find your house by myself.
   A) provided   B) if   C) because   D) including

3. Since I came to help you, I (　　) whatever you want me to do.
   A) have done   B) did   C) will do   D) doing

4. It was difficult to find the spot (　　) we buried our time capsule on our graduation day.
   A) what   B) where   C) which   D) who

5. The man (　　) with his eyes closed on the sidewalk after the accident.
   A) lied   B) laid   C) lay   D) lying

6. The men were brought in on a (　　) of conspiracy to kidnap the boy.
   A) discussion   B) charge   C) sin   D) punishment

7. It (　　) likely to rain, I decided not to go out.
   A) is   B) be   C) been   D) being

8. We were disturbed by the man's bad behavior, and so (　　) his wife.
   A) was   B) does   C) has   D) have

9. Your way of talking reminds me (　　) your mother.
   A) of   B) that   C) to   D) about

10. Lisa didn't feel at ease until the door was (　　) locked.
    A) secure   B) security   C) securely   D) secured

Appendix 1
Writing Guide: Format, Transitions & Punctuation

1) パラグラフの型の例

2) パラグラフからエッセイへ

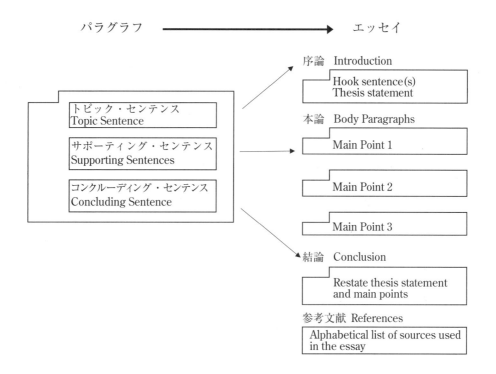

3) Five-paragraph Essay

大学の課題としてのエッセイ・ライティングで、"A" など高い評価を得たい場合は、本論で論じるトピックを3つ挙げ、全体で5つの paragraph を展開して内容を充実させることが、鍵となる。

4）Transitions（つなぎ語）の例

理由・原因	as; since; because (of); due to; now (that); owing to; thanks to など
結果	and; as a result; hence; so; therefore など
譲歩	after all; although; even if; even though; however; in spite of; nevertheless; regardless of; no matter; yet　など
条件・仮定	as (so) long as; if; provided (that); suppose/supposing; unless　など
強調	above all; certainly; indeed; of course; surely; truly　など
例示	especially; for example; for instance; specifically; thus　など
説明	in addition; furthermore; in other words; in this case; in fact; namely; that is; thus　　など
追加	also; besides that; in addition; moreover; then　など
類似点	also; both; in the same way; likewise; similarly　など
対照点	but; in contrast; on the other hand; instead; however; unlike; yet; whereas; while　など
要約	at last; finally; in a word; in conclusion; in general; in short; in summary; to sum up; to summarize　など
時間順	first; second; then; after all; after that; at last; finally; in the end; lastly; next; once; while　など
制限	as (so) far as; at least　など

5）Punctuation（句読法）

　　句読法とは、文章を構成するうえで伝えたいことが読者によく分かるようにするための符号のこと。特によく使われる句読点の基本的なルールを下の表に示してある。

「.」	period（ピリオド　フルストップ）	1）文章の終わりにつける。文章が完結したことを表す。 2）略語の省略記号として使われる。
「,」	comma（カンマ、コンマ）	1）2つ以上の独立節を結ぶ等位接続詞 (and, but, for, yet, so, or, no) の前につける。 2）等位接続詞を使用して3つ以上のものを並べるときに使われる。 　　Example: California, Oregon, and Washington are states that lie along the west coast of the USA. 3）接続詞などのつなぎ語の前後に使われる。 　　Example: Diamond is a rare and costly stone. Quartz, on the other hand, is abundant and cheap. 4）導入節や挿入句の後につける。 　　Example: Much more, of course, could be said. Thanks to the doctor's work, at least 300 children were saved.
「：」	colon（コロン）	1）例を列挙する場合に使われる。 2）主節で述べたことを別の表現で言い換える場合に使用される。 3）時間の表示や、本や記事のタイトルとサブタイトルを分けるのに使用される。
「;」	semicolon（セミコロン）	セミコロンは，コンマよりもピリオドに近い。 1）意味上関連する2つの文の間につける。 2）すでにコンマを含む語句が並立している場合に使用される。

「" "」 「' '」	quotation mark （クォーテー ション・マーク）	1) 引用文につける。その際、必ず引用部分の著者名を明記する必要がある。 Example: Brown has asserted, "It is possible to divide white-collar workers into specific categories according to their skill" (2010, p. 254). 2) エッセイや、短編小説、詩、歌詞、記事などのタイトルを引用するときにつける。 Example: Have you ever read Akutagawa's short story, "Rashomon"? 3) 引用文の中に、さらに引用が必要な場合につける。 Example: Mary said, "Maybe it would help us not to dislike cockroaches so much if we think of them as beetles. Like, 'Hey, Jude...'" 4) ある言葉自体を定義づけたり、皮肉的に用いる場合に使われる。 Example: I was immediately aware of my ignorance of the real meaning of the word "well-behaved."
「—」	Em-dash （ダッシュ）	1) 補足的な説明を、他の部分と区別するためにつける。 Example: However, Dr. Weiss administered the vaccine—vaccine that saved their lives! 2) それまでに述べたことの要約や、結論を書く場合に使う。（通常、ダッシュの後の部分は前の分より長くなる） Example: Prague is an ancient city—the impressive castle was founded in 870, and became the residence of the King of Bohemia during the 11th century.
「 - 」	hyphen （ハイフン）	1) 行の右端で単語が途中入りきらない場合、ハイフンで区切り、2行に分けて書く。（単語をどこで区切るのか、辞書で確認すること） Example: When the school bell rang at 12:30, the child- ren rushed outside to play. 2) 2つ以上の単語をつないで複合語を作る場合に用いる。 Example: The position may be full-time or part-time.
「–」	En-dash （ダッシュ）	Em-dash と Hyphen の間の長さで、距離・時間の間隔を書くときに使う。 Example: 1) We will stay in Kyoto from May 5 – 8. 2) The Tokyo – Yokohama train runs every ten minutes.

Appendix 1   73

Appendix 2
How to Organize an Effective Essay Outline

| **Brainstorming** ⇒ Listing ⇒ Clustering ⇒ Write Outline ⇒ Write Draft |
| ↑↑↑↑↑↑ |
| データの取捨選択 |

1) Brainstorming: エッセイを書き始める前の情報の整理。頭の中を活性化し、アイディアを生み出す。
2) Listing: トピックに関して、brainstorming で浮かんだことをすべて書き出してみる。
3) Clustering: トピックを基軸として図式化してみる。アイディアの上位概念、下位概念が明快に分かってくる。

Clustering の図

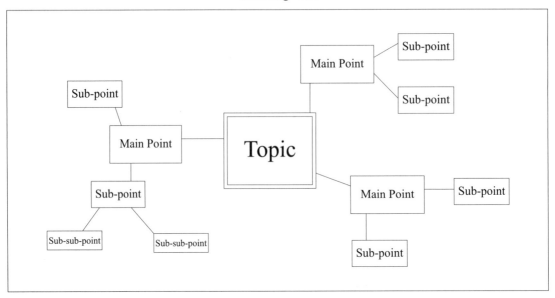

☆ データ整理：取捨選択して不要なものは捨てる。
☆ タイトルの決定。
☆ Five-paragraph essay の形にするとよい。

4) **Write Outline**: アウトラインの作成

I. 序論　**Introduction**
　　　　　　A. Hook sentence(s)
　　　　　　B. Main idea sentence(s)
　　　　　　C. Thesis statement

II. 本論　**Main point 1: paragraph 1**
　　　　　　A. Sub-point 1-1
　　　　　　B. Sub-point 1-2

III. 本論　**Main point 2: paragraph 2**
　　　　　　A. Sub-point 2-1
　　　　　　B. Sub-point 2-2

IV. 本論　**Main point 3: paragraph 3**
　　　　　　A. Sub-point 3-1
　　　　　　B. Sub-point 3-2

V. 結論　**Conclusion**
　　　　　　A. Restate thesis statement
　　　　　　B. Tie everything together

☆　**Hook sentence(s)** とは読者の興味をひくための文章 (Thesis statement へと導く部分)

☆　**Thesis statement** は、このエッセイのテーマを述べた文、主題文のこと。

☆　**Conclusion** は 1) Thesis statement を言葉を変えて強調する。
　　　　　　　2) Thesis statement と Main points を関連づける。

Appendix 3
Quotation Usage, Avoiding Plagiarism & Citation Methods

1) 剽窃とは

他人の著作から，credit（出典）を示すことなく文章の一部、語句や思想などを盗み、自分のものとして取り込むこと。

自分が知らなかった情報やどこかで得た内容について書く場合、その情報源を引用する必要がある。以下の場合は、情報源である著者の名前や出典を明記すること。

1) 直接引用（一語一句そのままを書く場合。" "を使う）

2) 書き換えたり、他者のアイディアを要約したりする。

引用しなければ剽窃になり、社会的な信用を失う場合がある。

2) なぜ引用や参照が必要か

引用を示す理由 (Turabian, 2007, 133-134)

1) 自分が使ったデータや事実の典拠を示すことで、自分の研究の客観性を示す。

2) 論文に関する研究の流れを示すことで、研究分野での論文の位置を明らかにする。

3) 読者が今後この分野で研究を進めるための手がかりを提供する。

4) これまでの先行研究や文献の功績を認める。

3) 引用の書き方

読者が最後の references（引用文献）を参照できるように、本文中の引用した情報の後に、（　　）内に著者の名前、年号等を入れる。引用スタイルは、MLA や APA スタイルなどがあるが、ここでは **APA style** を紹介する。

☆備考：以下に示されている引用は全て架空のものである。

4）**APA style** テキスト内の引用例

著者の名前	引用例
本文内での著者の名前 （括弧内に年号のみ）	Tanaka and Sato (2018) found that playing sports regularly improves language ability.
本文内に著者の名前が出ない場合（括弧内に名前と年号）	One study found that playing sports regularly improves language ability (Tanaka & Sato, 2018).
複数の出典（各出典をセミコロンで分ける）	Research shows that playing sports regularly improves language ability (Tanaka & Sato, 2018; Baker & Davis, 2015).
直接引用、本文内での著者の名前（ページ番号も必要）	Tanaka and Sato (2018) found that "language ability can be enhanced through regular engagement in physical activity" (p. 124).
直接引用、本文内に著者の名前が出ない場合	One study found that "language ability can be enhanced through regular engagement in physical activity" (Tanaka & Sato, 2018, p. 124).

5）**APA style** 引用文献例（論文の最後に全ての引用文献を記載する。）

a. Online Newspapers

Richardson, S. (2017, May 15). Students protest new graduation requirements, *Nippon News*. Retrieved: http://nipponnews.co.jp/30001/students-protest-new-graduation-requirements/ [2018, June 1].

b. Newspaper article with no author

Farmers welcome local support. (2010, September 4). *Tochigi Times*, p. 3.

c. Article with no date

Treater, J. (n.d.). How to write citations, *The Citation Page*, pp. 2-4.

d. Journal articles

Harlow, M. (2005). ESL students may benefit from intensive writing, *Journal of Language Educators*, 65(1), 150-165.

e. Books

Reston, H., & Meyers, M. (2012). *Best academic writing practices*. London: English Language Foundation.

f. Internet sources

Company/Organization Name. (Year). Title of page. Retrieved: URL [Month read date read, year read].

Appendix 3　　77

International Peace Association. (2016). World peace starts locally. Retrieved: http://www.interna
     tionalpeaceassociation.org/weekly.jhtml?id=415 [January 5, 2017].

☆ Wikipedia は、academic paper では引用文献として認めらない。以下は参考として示す。

g. Wiki

World diamond sites. (2017). Retrieved from the University of Imagination Wiki:
     http://imagination.wikia.com/wiki/World_Heritage_Sites [July 2, 2018].

h. Blog

Okamoto, V. (2016, August 3). A coffee a day: Keep the doctor away with caffeine. In *Drink to*
     your Health: Beverages to Soothe the Soul. Retrieved:
     http://drinktoyourhealth.com/blog/?p=142 [July 2, 2014].

6) **Reference List**（引用文献）の書き方

1. 引用文献はアルファベット順に並べる。
2. 各引用文献の二行目以降は、５スペース分インデントする。

References

Farmers welcome local support. (2010, September 4). *Tochigi Times*, p. 3.

Harlow, M. (2005). ESL students may benefit from intensive writing, *Journal of Language*
     Educators, 65(1), 150-165.

International Peace Association. (2016). World peace starts locally. Retrieved:
     http://www.internationalpeaceassociation.org/weekly.jhtml?id=415 [January 5, 2017].

Richardson, S. (2017, May 15). Students protest new graduation requirements, *Nippon News*.
     Retrieved: http://nipponnews.co.jp/30001/students-protest-new-graduation-requirements/
     [2018, June 1].

Appendix 4
Self-checklists

1) Self-checklist for Paragraphs

		Yes	No
内容（Content）			
	内容はトピック（主題）に関連している。		
	サポーティング・センテンスはトピックを十分に支持している。		
	主題の情報量が十分である。		
構成（Organization）			
	トピック・センテンスが明記されている。		
	複数のサポーティング・センテンスがある。		
	コンクルーディング・センテンスはトピック・センテンスと同じ内容になっている。		
	繋ぎ語を効果的に使っている。		
語彙（Vocabulary）			
	幅広い語彙を使用している。		
	同じ語彙を何度も使用していない。		
	効果的な語、イディオムを選択している。		
文法（Language Use）			
	主語と動詞の一致に関して誤りがない。		
	時制の一致に関して誤りがない。		
	冠詞、代名詞、前置詞等に関して誤りがない。		
綴り、句読点（Mechanics）			
	パラグラフはインデントされている。		
	綴り、句読点、大文字使用に関して誤りがない。		

ESL Composition Profile を参考に作成

Hughey, J. B., Wormuth, D. R., Hartfiel, V. F., & Jacobs, H. L.(1983). *Teaching ESL Composition Principles and Techniques*. Rowley: Newbury House.

2）Self-checklist for Essays

		Yes	No
内容 （Content）			
	タイトルはエッセイにふさわしい。		
	エッセイの中で主題を十分に発展させている。		
	十分な客観的資料を基にしている。		
	エッセイとして課された情報量が十分である。		
構成 （Organization）			
	序論 − 本論 − 結論 の構成になっている。		
	序論部分は興味深いフック・センテンスで始まっている。		
	序論部分にシーシス・ステイトメントが書かれている。		
	結論では、シーシス・ステイトメントとメイン・ポイントを言い換えている。		
首尾一貫性 （Coherence）			
	論旨はエッセイ全体を通して、首尾一貫して展開している。		
	序論に書かれていない内容を結論に加えない。		
	途中で、論旨 / 自分の意見（賛成か反対か）を変えない。		
	論旨が論理的に流れるように繋ぎ語を効果的に使っている。		
引用 （Citation）			
	引用の仕方は適切である。		
	剽窃部分はない。		
参考文献 （References）			
	References は全て明記した。		
	References はアルファベット順に書かれている。		

References

Hughey, J. B., Wormuth, D. R., Hartfiel, V. F., & Jacobs, H. L.(1983). *Teaching ESL Composition Principles and Techniques*. Rowley: Newbury House.

Kaplan, R. (1966). *Cultural thought patterns in intercultural education, Language Learning*, 16. 1-20.

Turabian, K. L. (2007). *A Manual for Writers of Research Papers, Theses, and Dissertations: Chicago Style for Students and Researchers. 7th ed.* Chicago: University of Chicago Press.

Yoshimura, T., Miwa, Y., Nishida, H. and Nakata, T. (2003). *Internet eigo gakushu-cho.* (*Handbook for Internet English Study*) Kyoto: Kitaoji-shobo.

挿絵：内　山　弘　隆

DONALD J. SOBOL
Solve the Mystery and Improve Your English Skills 3
ミステリーを読んで英語のスキルアップ3

2019 年 1 月 15 日　初　版

	吉　村　俊　子
	時　岡　ゆかり
	Susan E. Jones
編　著　者ⓒ	平　田　三　樹　子
	Jennifer Teeter
	伊　藤　佳世子

発　行　者　佐　々　木　　　元

発　行　所　株式会社　英　　宝　　社
〒101-0032 東京都千代田区岩本町 2-7-7
☎ [03] (5833) 5870　Fax [03] (5833) 5872

ISBN 978-4-269-02151-8 C1082
印刷・製本：モリモト印刷株式会社

本テキストの一部または全部を、コピー、スキャン、デジタル化等での
無断複写・複製は、著作権法上での例外を除き禁じられています。
本テキストを代行業者等の第三者に依頼してのスキャンやデジタル化は、
たとえ個人や家庭内での利用であっても著作権侵害となり、著作権法上
一切認められておりません。